Ways and Places to Sponsor New Distributors

*Discover Hot Prospects For Your
Network Marketing Business*

KEITH & TOM "BIG AL" SCHREITER

For information, contact:

Fortune Network Publishing
PO Box 890084
Houston, TX 77289 USA

Telephone: +1 (281) 280-9800

ISBN: 1-892366-45-2

ISBN-13: 978-1-892366-45-0

DEDICATION

This book is dedicated to network marketers everywhere.

I travel the world 240+ days each year. Let me know if you want me to stop in your area and conduct a live Big Al training.

http://www.BigAlSeminars.com

Get 7 mini-reports of amazing, easy sentences that create new, hot prospects.

Sign up today at:
http://www.BigAlReport.com

Other great Big Al Books available at:
http://www.BigAlBooks.com

TABLE OF CONTENTS

#1. Busy people. 9

#2. Get prospects to line up at your booth or display. 11

#3. Social media. 14

#4. Clerks. 21

#5. Networking events. 23

#6. Instant prospects and web traffic. 27

#7. How to get some quick success. 29

#8. Get their home address. 32

#9. Locate the fishing hole. 34

#10. Misfits. 39

#11. Trained salesmen. 40

#12. Turn losers into winners. 41

#13. The stair-step prospecting method. 43

#14. Turn a cold prospect into an entrepreneur. 52

#15. Put your message in your prospect's face. 53

#16. Sometimes simpler is better. 55

#17. The tax season approach. 56

#18. How to build a great prospect list for next year. 57

#19. A jar of jellybeans. 59

#20. Get your prospect to recruit immediately. 61

#21. Use a "grabber." 62

#22. How to meet people at parties. 64

#23. Start your own association. 66

#24. How to get people to ask you for a prospecting tool. ...68

#25. Let a charity find you fresh leads. 69

#26. Cruel and unusual punishment. 73

#27. Use gift certificates to lock in prospects. 74

#28. Free dinner premium to get a new product user. 76

#29. Catching fish in a fishbowl. 77

#30. Think global - work local. 85

#31. Choose your seat. 87

#32. Real estate agents. 88

#33. A subtle prospecting tool. 91

#34. Where to get a list of entrepreneurs who are workers! .94

#35. Think outside the box. 96

#36. How to stand out from your competition. 98

#37. Become a walking billboard. 99

#38. How to use a "bird dog" without being a hunter. 108

#39. Captive audiences. 112

#40. Immerse your prospects. 114

#41. Secret ad kept my phone ringing all day. 117

#42. Sponsor a Fun Run. 125

#43. How to build a downline in a foreign market............. 127

#44. Have your products delivered to your job. 130

#45. Throw a promotion party! 131

#46. How to get 300+ prospects willing to listen to you.... 134

#47. The best people. 136

#48. The people you know. 139

#49. Make sure your business card "sells." 142

#50. How to get more local prospects. 146

#51. Who sells to my prospects? 148

#52. Bonus! Just meet new people!................................... 156

PREFACE

Where do we find motivated prospects?

Easy. Great prospects are everywhere.

We just have to learn how and where to find them. The good news? Locating good prospects is one of the easiest skills in network marketing.

The following 51 ways and places will get you started.

Will you use all of these different ways? Of course not.

Some of these ways and places will fit your personality and comfort zone. Other ways may not. Your downline members might have different preferences than you. Perhaps they feel more comfortable locating their best prospects using different techniques.

Many of these sources of prospects can be used immediately, some are long-term, and a few are much bigger campaigns.

—Keith Schreiter and Tom "Big Al" Schreiter

#1. Busy people.

Everyone with a full-time job plus a part-time job qualifies as a great prospect for your business.

Why?

* They have motivation.

* They want a better financial future.

* They don't want to work two jobs the rest of their lives.

* And, they are taking action already by working those two jobs.

These prospects are everywhere, and many are eager for a change.

If you can't find someone who works a full-time job plus a part-time job, then ask for referrals. Just say to someone, "Who do you know who works a full-time job and a part-time job?" Many people can send you directly to these hard workers.

But what if they reply, "Why do you want to know?"

Here is your answer: "I want to help them get rid of at least one of those jobs so they have more time in their lives."

Once you find prospects who work a full-time job plus a part-time job, you'll often find they are surrounded with several co-workers who are doing the same. Now you have plenty of new, motivated prospects with a reason to change their lives.

#2. Get prospects to line up at your booth or display.

Go to a trade show, shopping center, or other location where networkers promote their programs and products. Many distributors spend a fortune passing out expensive literature and samples that prospects will never read or use. I've seen distributors waste $50 to $100 an hour with free giveaways.

Want a less expensive alternative that will get prospects to line up at your display? Wouldn't it be nice to have a captive audience of prospects waiting in line?

Here's how.

Hire a masseuse. Offer free five-minute back and neck massages, then watch the lines form. You will have plenty of time to visit with prospects while they stand in line and wait for their turn.

The cost?

Maybe you can hire a masseuse for $40 or $50 an hour. Or what about a masseuse student at even lower rates?

Now this is inexpensive marketing. You will guarantee a long line of prospects at your location. You can be sure you will be the hit of the trade show or shopping center!

Want to go the cheaper route?

Buy an electric foot massager for a few hundred dollars. Bring a folding chair to your booth for people to sit. Put up a sign:

"FREE 5-Minute Foot Massage!"

And now you have a captive audience for at least five minutes. Plus, you can talk to the people standing in line.

Trade show tip.

If you have a trade show booth, you know that people collect literature. You could be just another vendor they will ignore when you do your follow-up call.

Here is how to distinguish yourself from the crowd.

A few days before the trade show, hand-write some postcards thanking a person for stopping by your booth. Take these postcards to the show.

At the end of the day, handwrite in the name and address of the prospects who visited your booth. Then, drop the postcards into the mail.

Your prospects might receive the postcard the next day! Handwritten postcards look and feel so personal. You know your follow-up phone call will be better received.

Here's a hint to make it even better.

Make your postcard a picture postcard. One side of the postcard can be a full-color picture of something humorous, something that sells your product, or something that maybe sells <u>you</u>.

You need to stand out in a crowd, and this is one way to do it.

#3. Social media.

Social media is ... **social**. Most people don't want us blasting our daily offers and product features on our personal Facebook page, Twitter feed, etc.

But social media is also good to build rapport. People get to know us and they feel closer to us, unlike a cold prospect.

Platforms such as Facebook, LinkedIn, Twitter, etc. are always changing the rules, so your marketing tactics will always be changing.

Instead of worrying about the latest changes of your favorite social media platforms, concentrate on a simple "big picture" strategy.

A simple **part-time** social media strategy could be as simple as:

"Make three new contacts a day."

Pretty simple. But over time, our warm market expands. In this example, with just three new contacts a day, we would have over 1,000 new people who know us in just one year. That's over 5,000 people who know us over the next five years.

Now, with 1,000 to 5,000 new contacts, sponsoring is easy. For many in this list, the timing is right for them now. They will have experiences throughout the year that will motivate them to look for change. That change could be your business opportunity.

And that is all it takes in network marketing. Sponsor a few of these people, and teach them to do the same.

Out of 1,000 or even 5,000 people, many of them would be looking for a change on any given day. It would be easy if we said the right words. And of course, we can learn the right words.

But how will we get these new people to engage with us? Of course we could provide tips and content, but let's make this a bit more interesting. Here is just one way to get started.

Create a riddle that is challenging and viral.

For example, if you sold nutritional products you could create a test like this:

Which food will kill you fastest?

A. Donuts.

B. German chocolate cake.

C. Pizza.

D. Ice cream.

Click HERE for the answer.

*****

15

(It's only an example. I just made this test up using my four favorite food groups.) You would want to place a link to the answer, and make sure you had some selling copy on that landing page.

This sample test would be viral since many people would send it to their friends. That means extra exposure to qualified prospects that you couldn't reach yourself.

What other types of riddles could I use?

Want prospects for your business? Try this riddle.

Which choice best describes your boss?

A. Dream-sucking vampire.

B. Selfish, egotistical jerk.

C. Life-crusher.

D. Pompous know-it-all self-absorbed narcissist.

Vote now, then click HERE to see how others have voted.

*****

When they go to the landing page to see how others voted, give them an opportunity to look at your business.

Better yet, ask them to enter a contest by describing how bad their boss is in 200 words or less. First prize? An interview with you to show them how to leave their job.

Or, how about this?

Which is the quickest way to poverty?

A. Buying lottery tickets.

B. Dead-end job.

C. Internet-surfing addiction.

D. Watching inflation eat away at your savings account.

Click HERE for the answer.

*****

Want to be a bit more on the edge?

Let's create a simple test for the misery of job insecurity:

Which is the worst scenario when you arrive at work?

A. The boss says, "Oh, leave your coat on."

B. Your cubicle is replaced with filing cabinets.

C. Your co-workers look away as you walk in.

D. The parking lot is empty.

Click HERE for the answer.

*****

Now, this is starting to get fun. What else could we do? Try this one:

How much more does your boss earn for working the same number of hours that you work?

A. 10%

B. 25%

C. 50%

D. 300%

Click HERE for the answer.

*****

Does your audience have a warped sense of humor?

Imagine your perfect prospect is someone dissatisfied with working for a miserable boss. You might get away with this survey:

Which animal best describes your boss?

A. Blood-sucking leech.

B. Vampire bat.

C. Lazy, three-toed sloth.

D. Pack rat.

Click HERE for the answer.

*****

Remember to have a good landing page when they click for the answer. Want another example?

Rich people pay what percentage of their income in taxes?

A. 0%

B. 10%

C. 50%

D. 75%

Click HERE for the answer.

*****

Need a simple test for skincare products?

Which product will make your skin wrinkle the most?

A. Soap.

B. Facial cleanser.

C. Sunscreen.

D. Mineral oil.

Click HERE for the answer.

*****

How about this to engage prospects who love to travel?

Which is the most popular destination for travelers?

A. Tahiti.

B. Paris.

C. Hawaii.

D. North Dakota.

Click HERE for the answer.

*****

Yes, social media is ... social.

Social media is also fun. But at the same time, you can be building your network of interested, qualified prospects.   .

When you engage prospects, they step forward and volunteer. It is easier to market to a list of quality prospects that love what you do, and have some history with you also. You won't be a stranger.

There are plenty of books written about social media. New social media opportunities are announced daily. Strategies must constantly be adjusted to the ever-changing rules.

But to start, just keep the big picture in mind. A few new contacts each day adds up over time.

#4. Clerks.

Just stop to put fuel in your car. And don't pay at the pump!

Inside the building is a clerk. What do we know about this clerk?

1. The clerk likes money. Hey, the clerk is working, right?

2. The clerk is responsible. Somebody trusts the clerk to handle money.

3. The clerk is underpaid. I have never seen an overpaid clerk.

4. The clerk hates the job. It is boring, especially on the night shift.

5. The clerk hates being target practice for criminals at night while protecting his boss' money.*

Say something like this to the clerk (remembering the rule of disagreement):

"Hey, this looks like a pretty nice job. You get to work inside and you don't have to worry about nasty weather."

The clerk will usually **disagree** and now your conversation begins. Easy, isn't it?

All you have to do then is use your favorite "Ice Breaker" and let the fun begin.

If you want more prospects, don't fill up your fuel tank at one station. Instead, stop at several fuel stations and only do partial fill-ups.

*Always use your judgment on which locations and what time to visit.

#5. Networking events.

Many years ago, Bob and Anna Bassett from Canada shared their "Five-Question Test." They told me the story of their friend, Herbie.

Herbie would be talking to a prospect at a networking event, and then suddenly, turn and walk away, sometimes in mid-sentence. When asked about the abrupt behavior, Herbie answered,

"Well, he didn't pass the Five-Question Test."

What's the Five-Question Test?

Herbie explained, "Well, when I meet somebody new, I try to learn as much as I can about him by asking questions. I ask him five questions during our conversation, and if he hasn't asked me anything, then I know he is only interested in himself. I just walk away. There is no point in talking to anyone who doesn't pass the Five-Question Test."

Prospecting isn't all about you.
It is all about the prospects.

Don't start by talking all about you and your company. Soon no one will be listening. Instead, learn as much as you can about your prospects.

Find out if they have a problem you can solve. Build a relationship with them. Then, when they decide to solve their problem, they will choose to solve it with you.

It doesn't matter if your prospects pass the Five-Question Test. What matters is that **you** pass the Five-Question Test.

What your prospect wants to hear.

Copywriter Bill Jayne says it all in the following quote:

"It doesn't matter what you are selling. Your direct marketing should never be about the product. It should always be about the prospect."

So ask yourself:

* How much of your current opportunity presentation is about your company, products, and compensation plan?

* How much of your current opportunity presentation is about your prospect?

Great recruiters know that their presentation should be about the prospect's favorite subject: the prospect.

So you might think, "Sounds good, but how do I get them to talk about wanting my business?"

Try some closing questions to get the prospects to think about getting solutions to their problems. It is amazing how interested prospects are in our business when it is their idea.

Here are a few questions you can use:

* Are you okay with not having enough time for holidays and family?

* That is a long commute every day. What do you do during those two hours?

* I am just curious, how hard is it to get a decent raise where you work?

Immediately the conversation shifts to the prospect wanting a business or better opportunity.

Why some people are natural attractions at networking events.

You go to a business networking event. Everyone pushes their business card in your hand. Gives you their prepared sales pitch. Then they rush off to the next victim.

Everyone leaves with a stack of business cards of people they will never call. Ouch.

Here is a famous quote by Frederick Collins that instantly makes you a natural attraction at networking events:

"There are two types of people. Those who come into a room and say, 'Well, here I am.' And those who come in and say, 'Ah, there you are.'"

That is the difference between a professional networker and a cheesy, pushy salesman at networking events.

Try it.

It is better to have a good working relationship with just a few people, than a fistful of business cards from people you'll never hear from again.

#6. Instant prospects and web traffic.

Don't complain about not having prospects or non-existent website traffic. There are opportunities everywhere.

I was in Yellowstone Park, surrounded by tourists. My cellphone took better pictures than most expensive cameras did. To create prospects and drive traffic to my website, all I had to do was:

1. Offer to take the picture of a tourist family. Most of the time it was after a "selfie fail."

2. Tell them that I would be glad to email the picture to them.

3. Email the picture to them with a short message and a teaser signature file at the end of the message that would compel them to check out my website. Not familiar with a signature file? It is like a P.S. that is automatically added to the end of your email messages. The teaser message could be as simple as:

* Do you remember what I look like? Click here to see my picture.

* Click here to see my before and after picture. What do you think?

27

* Click here to see a picture of what I really do.

* Click here to see if you look like my boss.

* Click here to see a picture of the new car I won.

* Click here to see how much weight I lost this month.

* Is your paycheck a disgrace? Click here.

* Click here to see how I get one extra paycheck every month.

* Click here to see a picture of my dog biting my ...

* Click here to read my daughter's opinion.

* Click here to learn why I turned out how my mother predicted.

Instant prospects. Instant web traffic. Cost = zero.

This is easier than approaching strangers on their vacation and asking them, "Do you want to earn some extra money?"

My results? Almost every tourist family wanted their picture and gladly gave me their email address.

So make sure your webpage is ready for the influx of vacationers who want a better life.

#7. How to get some quick success.

Everyone wants instant results and gratification. Waiting for momentum to build is frustrating. So let's look at how we can kick-start our business with a lot of new distributors fast.

The core asset a person brings to network marketing is their contact list. Some people have spent years building contacts, relationships, customers and a network of influencers. Their warm market of prospects that they can contact is huge.

Even better, their contacts respect them, and will happily take their advice. When these connected influencers join your business, it is easy for them to enroll their warm market quickly. You will experience quick results and your downline will build momentum. It will seem to others that everyone wants to join. Social proof will help those fence-sitters make a decision to join now.

Who are these connected individuals with contacts, relationships, customers and a network of influencers? Let's look at some examples.

1. Insurance agents. Many families have put their financial plans into the hands of a trusted insurance agent.

2. Community volunteers. Volunteers spend their time helping others. Their friends trust that their intentions are

pure. When a community volunteer talks, people listen and trust their motives.

3. Policemen. They come in contact with hundreds of people. Most people respect policemen. They are underpaid for risking their lives. Their families worry about their safety. Policemen have many incentives to join your business.

4. Politicians. Talk about influence! They are professional influencers and prove it every election cycle.

5. Wedding planners. They get things done. Their execution must be perfect or the bride will complain. But think of how many people they know and contract with. The list of people they know is huge.

6. Firemen. Some firemen work 48 hours on and the rest of the week off. This gives them time for two careers, and two sets of contacts just from their work. Prospects respect firemen.

7. Salesmen. Do salesmen know a lot of people? Of course. When the salesman has good rapport skills, the salesman will have a huge prospect list that could take months to contact.

8. Active mothers. Think of mothers who are active in their children's school, the local neighborhood association, and social clubs. Most women have a huge network of other women. When they need to source out bargains or hard-to-find items, they simply put the word out to their extended networks.

9. Personal trainers and fitness instructors. They interact with their client list weekly.

10. Doctors and health professionals. When you trust someone to advise you on your health, well, trust doesn't get much deeper than that. You will listen to their proposals with an open mind.

What do all of these people have in common?

They are experienced networkers. They are already 50% on their way to success. They have prospects who will listen to them with open minds, and these prospects trust them also.

When you sponsor one of these experienced networkers, your appointment book fills instantly. When you help your new "experienced" networker, you will be busy for weeks. Your day will be filled with presentations and helping their new distributors talk to their lists of warm market prospects.

So if you need to get off to a faster start, contact experienced networkers who have a ready list of prospects.

#8. Get their home address.

Want to have more prospects ask you about your business? Try this:

Go to relatives, co-workers and friends, and ask them,

"What is your home address?"

Most will react by saying,

"Why do you want to know?"

Reply by saying,

"I am going on a one-week cruise for my business, and I want to send you a postcard."

And then, wait.

Most people will ask you about your business.

This is a great way to get lots of qualified prospects before you leave for your cruise.

If you are not going on a company cruise, maybe you will be going to your company regional convention. Then you would say:

"I am going to Phoenix for my business, and I wanted to send you a postcard."

And here is one more hint to help you enjoy your trip.

Since you will be sending back lots of postcards, prepare the address labels before you leave. Then, all you have to do is attach the label and write a short message when you arrive at your destination.

Many of your prospects will attach your picture postcard to their refrigerator or bulletin board at home. The picture will constantly remind them of you and your business opportunity.

#9. Locate the fishing hole.

A wide, shallow stream flows through the area. The stream is only ankle-deep. Further downstream is a lovely, deep, clear pool.

Today is your day to go fishing. Where would you cast your line? In the shallow, fast-moving stream? Or, would you cast your line in the deep pool that offers the fish both food and safety? (Hint: choose the second option.)

There are two rules for becoming a great fisherman:

Rule #1. Cast your line where the fish are.

Rule #2. Tell great stories about the one that got away.

Let's only talk about Rule #1 (Go fishing where the fish are) and how it applies to network marketing.

Here is where struggling networkers look for quality prospects:

* They place an ad that looks like a job. The prospects answer the ad looking for a job, not a business. Now the trust is broken even before a presentation begins.

* They ask their relatives to give up their bowling league night to come to a business opportunity meeting. Even if their relatives came, they wouldn't be happy.

* They stand on a street corner passing out product samples to disinterested pedestrians. These networkers hope the people passing by will use and fall in love with their product.

* They go to the unemployment office and announce, "Does anyone here want to lose their weekly benefits check? Please contact me about a business opportunity." The response is underwhelming.

These techniques are about as effective as throwing an alarm clock into a cemetery.

So where are the fish?

If you had a choice, you would go fishing where the fish are so thick you could practically walk across the pond. Why waste time fishing in places where the fish are scarce?

Elaborate, expensive recruiting campaigns are not the answer. The secret is simple: **creative** recruiting campaigns where all the prospects are great prospects!

Finding those incredible pre-sold prospects.

Many years ago, I sponsored a lady named Dorothy. She was a beautician, pigeon-holed into a limited earning potential. Even though she worked long hours with little free time, she knew network marketing was for her.

Her regular customers didn't want a long-term business with long-term rewards. They focused on today's soap operas. Why should they work today and wait to get paid months later? They preferred to get a paycheck even before they had to go to work! Not many fish in this pool of prospects for Dorothy. It just wasn't their time.

With only two nights a week free, where could Dorothy go to build a group of go-getters fast? We needed a plan.

First, we profiled the perfect prospect for Dorothy and her limited time. These are the qualities we wanted.

1. The prospects should have a job. Unemployed prospects need money fast. They need a **job**. They don't have time to wait for a **business** to build. When prospects don't have jobs, they don't have any extra money to join a business, to buy products, to get business cards or fund the other minimal expenses of creating a network marketing business.

2. The prospects should want to move forward in their lives. They should want raises, promotions, and a chance to be better in their working careers.

3. The prospects should be local. It is easier to present and train prospects over a cup of coffee or at a local meeting room. You can present your opportunity person-to-person, you can answer questions, build relationships, and bond with your new team.

4. The prospects should love selling. Dorothy didn't have enough free time to convince her prospects to love selling. We might as well hope for prospects who are already excited about selling.

Going where the action is.

Here was our solution.

The local Chamber of Commerce sponsored a series of free business classes in the evenings at a local university. Volunteers would teach classes in their fields of expertise for a few hours, one night a week, for six weeks.

You could learn accounting, management, and of course, selling. We chose the Tuesday night class to learn how to sell. This would only take up one evening of Dorothy's week. And since the class was free, we invited some of Dorothy's current distributors to join us. They could be learning about selling too, right?

Now, what did we know about our classmates?

1. Everyone had a job. That is why they had to go to night school to learn.

2. Everyone wanted to move forward in their lives. They had full-time jobs and now wanted to learn new skills.

3. Everyone was local. Nobody would fly into town once a week to go to a night class.

4. Everyone in the class loved to sell. They were salesmen already, or planned to be future salesmen. They volunteered to take a class on learning how to sell even better!

Shooting fish in a barrel.

Sponsoring classmates was easy. Everyone wanted to earn more, wanted to invest in themselves to move forward. They saw that the benefits of our business matched what they wanted in life.

1. They could create a steady monthly income instead of the ups and downs of commission selling. They could even get paid when they were sick and couldn't go out and make commission sales.

2. They could grow the business to be as large as they wanted.

3. They could be their own boss.

4. No risk. They didn't have to invest big money. All they had to do was invest some time and energy. They didn't have to risk their family's savings account with a big business investment.

The payoff?

Most of the class members (37 out of the 42 in the class) enrolled as distributors or customers. And don't forget the instructor!

We have to go fishing where there are fish, qualified fish. No matter how good your offer might be, if your prospects don't qualify, or if it is not the right time for them, you are fishing in the wrong spot.

#10. Misfits.

Some people just don't fit in well with a job. They like to do things "their way." The result? They get fired. These people feel they know better, are smarter, or just enjoy thinking outside the box. Usually they are creative and would love to be their own boss and do things their way.

Wow. Sounds like they are great prospects to me!

How do you find these "misfits?" Just ask. Here is another opportunity to use your referral skills.

For example, go to the local fast food restaurant, find the manager, and ask, "Who did you fire recently for being too creative?" In some cases, you might get a long list.

Or, "Who used to work for you who was always making suggestions on how to do things better?"

Some people just have a unique way of doing things. Allow them to do it their way when they join your business. They will thank you for allowing them the freedom to be themselves.

#11. Trained salesmen.

Want high-quality, local prospects at no cost?

Go to a local merchant - but don't try to sell the merchant anything. Just ask for a favor.

Ask the merchant:

"Who are the best salespeople or representatives calling on you now?"

You may get names of terrific salespeople who hate their jobs and would welcome your opportunity. And because you are getting the names of the very best, you will have high-quality prospects that you can contact. Many of these salespeople would welcome a part-time income, and some may even want to be their own boss.

Be kind. Contact them, and give them one more option for their lives. They may thank you forever.

#12. Turn losers into winners.

Think marketing! A little imagination can go a long way.

For example, let's say you sold diet products and couldn't afford advertising. Maybe all you could afford for your promotion was one month's worth of diet products.

So what could you do? How about a contest for LOSERS?

Announce that anyone can enter your contest, but they must have two qualifications.

1. They must own a losing lottery ticket.

2. They must want to lose weight.

Hold a drawing of the submitted losing lottery tickets and give away a one-month supply of diet products to the winner.

You would get plenty of word-of-mouth advertising and publicity from such an innovative campaign. Make the campaign more interesting by holding the drawing at the local donut shop or pizzeria.

* If you sold skincare products, how about a "Lose those wrinkles" contest?

* If you sold travel services, how about a "Lose those winter blues" contest for people who hate winter?

* If you wanted to promote your business opportunity, how about a "Lose your boss" contest?

* Or how about this? See who could submit the best reason to "Lose your alarm clock." Wow. They would be ultra-qualified prospects.

#13. The stair-step prospecting method.

This is an intensive method, but if mastered, is one of the most productive recruiting campaigns imaginable.

Imagine if Big Al received a letter from a member in his group. The letter said:

Dear Big Al,

I am a new distributor just getting started in network marketing. I just moved to a new town and don't know anyone. I want to build a strong network marketing business. Since I have no experience in network marketing, I don't know where to start or what to do.

I won't ask for much, and I won't take much of your time. You don't have time to take on a protégé, so I will ask for only one favor.

*Would you please come down for **just one day**, and get me off to a quick start? Just teach me one technique and I will build my business from that starting point. I am a self-starter, so you will never have to hear from me again.*

That's it. Just give me one day and I will be forever in your debt.

Sincerely,

Jerry Aggressive (Brand-New Distributor)

What a letter!

What would you do if you got this letter? This motivated self-starter could really make your business grow. We enjoy getting letters from motivated people. All he wants is just **one little miracle!**

It is hard for a new distributor to build a group. It takes trial and error, workshops and training seminars, retailing, prospecting, leadership and more. Several months may pass with little or no progress. There will be ups and downs. Product shipments may be late. Meetings may be hard to organize. It will take time to build a large and dedicated group to have exciting meetings.

We have to build deep to help our new distributor taste some success. If our brand-new distributor knows nothing about our business, our task can be overwhelming.

Our new distributor wants a successful, excited, large organization of new distributors now. And he is generous; he is going to give us **one whole day** to work our miracle. He wants to bypass months of work to become an instant leader with an excited distributor organization.

Well, this is the challenge of leadership. Since new distributors hold us in high esteem, they **expect** us to work miracles.

So, what can we do for "one day" that will accomplish all of our new distributor's objectives? Do we run an ad? Tell him to make a few hundred new friends before we arrive? Do we put on a suit of armor and go door-to-door, begging people to become distributors? Or, how about giving the new distributor a catchy slogan on a lapel button?

We can tell our new distributor to walk around shopping malls and hope prospects will mob him with distributor applications. Maybe we could mail out flyers to strangers in the phone book and hope they send us orders and completed applications. With only one day to perform a miracle, we don't have many options.

So here is the test. **What would you do?** (Skipping town or faking illness is not an acceptable option. Your distributor wants a miracle.)

The stair-step solution.

Dear Jerry,

It is always a pleasure to hear from a motivated self-starter. I appreciate your attitude to go out on your own and be responsible for your financial future.

Yes, my schedule is tight and my open time is limited. However, I'm looking forward to this opportunity to help you get off to a great start. I appreciate your desire to learn streamlined and effective ways to build your business. Too many new distributors use trial and error to reinvent the wheel.

Here is my only requirement to help you for the day:

Make an appointment with three or four people to spend five minutes with me. Just tell them that I wish to talk with them about business. You may also tell them the name of our company or answer any other questions they may have. I only wish to ask them a few questions.

If you do your part, I will guarantee you will have up to 20 people in your organization in just a few days. We won't have enough time to get all 20 on the day I am with you. However, I will build the foundation and give you the technique to finish the job.

I am looking forward to our day together next week.

Sincerely,

Big Al

So, what happened?

The day of reckoning arrived. Big Al met Jerry and his first prospect at the local restaurant. His prospect, John, was a local businessman and a member of the Jaycees. He had welcomed Distributor Jerry to the community just a few days earlier.

Big Al asked John if he was familiar with network marketing. John was aware of this type of business and once attended an exciting opportunity meeting. The opportunity meeting lasted over two hours and John had to leave before it was over. He decided not to join because if a meeting took that long, there wouldn't be enough time to work the business.

Big Al explained a little about the company and how the meetings were only 30 minutes. John said he had enough time for some more details, so Big Al gave a quick 20-minute presentation.

At the end of the presentation, John said, "Very interesting. I will go home and think it over for a few days."

Then Big Al utilized the stair-step close.

"John, you know that Jerry is just opening up the opportunity in this area. We will put 20 new distributors into the organization over the next few days. We would like them all to be in your downline. This would give you a tremendous start and you could provide some good, stable leadership for them. Would you please give me the correct spelling of your last name and email address? Then, the next person we talk to can get you as his sponsor."

Big Al typed in the name and email in the sponsor section of the online application. Next, he asked John to fill in the remaining details. Jerry just stared in amazement. Finally, Big Al filled in the proper information for a product purchase so that John would have some experience with the product line.

Jerry wondered, "Why did John change his mind so quickly? Was it the promise of 20 people in his downline? How are we going to get 20 people to keep this commitment? We don't know anyone in this town."

When John finished the paperwork, Big Al said, "John, as you can see, this is a great opportunity. I know you probably have a close friend or business associate that you would like to help. As long as we are going to be building the organization of new distributors under you, maybe we should enroll your friend next. Then he will benefit also from this group of distributors."

John replied, "That is a great idea. My best friend Mike has always wanted to be in a part-time business and earn extra money. Your help in getting new distributors would get him off to a guaranteed fast start and build his confidence! Let's get him on the phone now and sign him up before you get the rest of the distributors."

John quickly called Mike. Mike asked that Big Al and Jerry hurry over to his house before he left for work. If John said it was a good deal, and there was a guaranteed quick start, he wanted to sign up now.

Big Al thanked John for his time. "Remember, the first meeting for this area is one week from today."

Big Al and Jerry jumped in Big Al's car and drove to Mike's house.

On the way over, Jerry commented, "That's incredible! The first person we talked to signed up, gave us a product order, and referred us to a pre-sold prospect. I think the promise of 20 distributors in his downline had a lot to do with it. What puzzles and bothers me is that you and I together know less than three people in this town. How are we going to keep our commitment?"

Big Al replied, "Observe closely, and see what your conclusions are at the end of the day. Let's visit Mike and see what we learn from him."

Mike was the easiest presentation Jerry could imagine. He was already mentally committed to join when he answered the doorbell. His respect for John and John's enthusiasm had completely pre-sold Mike before Big Al and Jerry arrived.

At the end of the brief presentation, Big Al said, "Mike, as John told you, we are concentrating on bringing in new distributors over the next few days. In fact, we are going to be putting 19 new distributors into your organization to give you a fast start. I am sure you have a friend or close business associate who would like to take advantage of this fast start. We could put distributors into his organization while still helping you. Your friend would thank you for this opportunity. Who do you know that deserves and would appreciate this fast start in his own part-time business?"

Mike quickly answered, "I've been thinking about that since my conversation with John earlier this morning. My brother, Jim, could be good in this business. I always wanted to help him get ahead, and this would be the perfect opportunity. Let me call him now and see if you can go right over. I want you to sign him up before you get the other new distributors. I want him up on top. He could be the next superstar for this company."

Mike's brother, Jim, said Big Al and Jerry could meet with him at work in 15 minutes. He could take a little break to visit with them and see what they had to offer.

Jim got excited about the help in building his downline and that John and Mike had already signed up.

Big Al closed by saying, "Jim, when it came down to one person that Mike wanted to help, he chose you. Mike knew that you would appreciate our efforts in giving you a fast start in building your downline. We plan to put 18 new distributors into your downline over the next few days. Who do you want at the top of your organization?"

Jim replied, "Big Al, there are two people that I feel would love the extra help you offer. First, my boss here at work. He is always looking to improve his finances. The other prospect is my next-door neighbor, Allen. Would it be possible for my boss to sponsor Allen, and you continue to build under Allen? That way your efforts would benefit not only me, but also my boss and Allen."

"No problem," said Big Al. He and Jerry went upstairs and introduced Jim's boss to the program. At the end of the presentation, Jim's boss wanted to think it over. Big Al said "We will need your name and social security number as the sponsor for Allen. Allen is Jim's next-door neighbor. Jim wanted you to be his sponsor so all of Allen's efforts would benefit you." Jim's boss filled out the application.

Before leaving to see Allen, Big Al said to Jim's boss, "Since we are going to put 17 new distributors into your organization over the next few days, who would you like to benefit from this effort? If you have a friend or close business associate that you would like at the top of these new distributors, let's talk to him right away so he benefits, too."

Jim's boss answered, "I appreciate that Jim wants me to sponsor his next-door neighbor, Allen. To show my appreciation, I am going to sponsor my three best friends under Allen. That way your recruiting efforts can continue under my three friends and benefit all of us. Let me get them on the phone and make the appointments."

And so the day went. By that evening, Big Al and Jerry had sponsored 14 new distributors. With only a few more distributors needed to reach his goal of 20, Jerry was confident that next week's first meeting was going to be great.

"I see how you keep your commitments to help people off to a fast start," said Jerry. "You can go home early. I can finish this job. I now have enough leads to finish up the remaining six distributors we need to fulfill our commitments. This simple technique will build me an organization beyond my wildest dreams. I only have one first-level distributor now, but there will be a total of 20 distributors in my group for next week's meeting. And everyone will be excited because they have distributors in their downline. I am not worried about having only one first level. Starting next week I am going to sponsor my second first-level distributor. And guess what? I will work with my next first level until he or she has 20 distributors in their downline also.

"Today was a miracle for me, Big Al. I saw 15 presentations, and 14 people joined. I now have a growing, excited organization. And all this in just one day! Now I see how an upline sponsor should work. I am going to follow your footsteps and show my organization how to do the same."

So Big Al left Jerry to finish up this recruiting campaign.

It's amazing what you can accomplish in **just one day.**

#14. Turn a cold prospect into an entrepreneur.

It takes just a minute or two, and is so easy.

Ask your prospect to:

1. Write down three things he likes to do.

2. Next, ask him to write down how much time he spends doing each of these things.

3. Ask the prospect, "Who is in charge of your time?"

4. If the prospect understands that he is in charge of his time, explain how network marketing can give the prospect more control over his life.

#15. Put your message in your prospect's face.

I had two guests coming to meet me at the diner for a presentation. Since I arrived early, there were a few minutes to wait.

I was bored, so I looked at the placemats – and they were blank!

What a waste of advertising space. Here is a great place to advertise and get your prospects' undivided attention. Few networkers take advantage of this resource.

Now think about the restaurant owner. He had to pay for these blank placemats. Maybe he goes through 5,000 or 10,000 placemats a month. It is not a huge expense, but it is an expense nonetheless.

You could print placemats with your advertisement and give them to the restaurant owner for free. The owner is happy. You get your advertisement in front of thousands of people for just a few dollars.

Will the restaurant owner take free placemats from you?

Of course. You have seen placemats at other restaurants with multiple ads. Someone gave these placemats to that local restaurant owner.

51 Ways and Places
To Sponsor New Distributors

But you can make it easier for the owner. Why not include a puzzle for the kids and some word games for the adults? Now the placemat has entertainment value.

Worried about the cost of printing placemats? Just co-op an ad or two with other businesses. Let them give you money to have their ads seen with yours. That should cover the minimal printing costs. Hmmm, that makes your ad free!

And finally, people like immediate gratification. So why not enroll the restaurant owner? Have the restaurant owner stockpile some of your products so your placemat ad could say:

"Just pick up some at the cash register on the way out."

This works great if you have a good ad that compels people to buy a product. With a little imagination, you could create a message or quiz on the placemat that could prime your prospect to look for a better opportunity.

#16. Sometimes simpler is better.

While talking to a distributor who sold healthy snacks, I asked her where she found her best prospects. She said:

"It is easy. At work, I simply follow people when they go to the snack vending machine. Then I stand next to them, eat my healthy snack, and they always ask me how they can get some healthy snacks too."

She is selling lots of healthy snacks and making a great part-time income at work.

Meanwhile, another distributor is doing this:

1. Creating a healthy snack brochure.

2. Designing the copy for the webpage.

3. Hiring someone to create the webpages.

4. Writing the autoresponder series.

5. Testing a Google Adwords keyword group.

6. Creating an order page, etc.

Sometimes we forget that network marketing is a people-to-people business.

#17. The tax season approach.

Train your tax preparer to say this to his clients.

After the client hands over his bookkeeping and receipts, the tax preparer should say:

"And what part-time business are you using this year to reduce your taxes? Most people don't want to pay the maximum amount of taxes from their salaried jobs."

The client will naturally want to know about starting a part-time business. The tax preparer could simply refer them to you.

* You win. You get a new distributor.

* The tax preparer wins. He gets a satisfied client, and if he is in your business, builds a downline for residual income during the rest of the year.

* The client wins. He gets a business, gets to take more tax deductions, and can start building a residual income.

#18. How to build a great prospect list for next year.

Not every prospect will join immediately after your presentation.

Why?

Maybe the timing is not right. Maybe they are still happy with their job or financial future. Or maybe they feel that their present plan to financial independence is working.

How do you motivate some of these prospects months after your initial presentation? Here's a way:

When your prospect declines to join your business, give the prospect a blank envelope and a form that says:

* The present balance of my checking account:

* The present balance of my savings account:

* The present balance of my credit cards:

* The present balance of my retirement account:

Ask the prospect to fill out this form in private and put it into the envelope. Have the prospect seal the envelope and put it in a safe place.

And finally, say this:

"Let's see how your present plan is working. Hopefully, it will give you the financial results you are looking for. Let's get together and check how your plan is working in about six months, okay?"

If your prospect is like most prospects, there will be no progress in six months. It will make your second visit a lot easier.

#19. A jar of jellybeans.

Let's say that you have a prospect that just doesn't see the value of your opportunity. You know this prospect could be great in your business. How can you get him to remember your business opportunity?

Give your special prospect a jar of jellybeans.

Create a label that says,

"For temporary stress relief from unreasonable bosses. Take two beans every four hours until the problem goes away. If problem persists, call John Doe at xxx-xxx-xxxx to start your own home-based business."

When your prospect has that jar of jellybeans on his desk, he sees it every day and thinks about you. So, when the time is right for the prospect, your prospect will be thinking about you.

Only a little bit mean …

Interested in taking this idea a little farther? Let a miserable jar of jellybeans eat away at your prospect's brain. Here's how it works.

Imagine your prospect has 20 years before retirement. That is approximately 5,000 more days of work. Yes, 5,000 days!

Buy a big jar of 5,000 jellybeans. Give it to your good prospect as a gift with the instructions:

"Each jellybean represents one day of your life, working for someone else. All you have to do is eat one jellybean each morning when you come to work. That's it! When you finish eating this jar of jellybeans, your life is just about over. Hopefully then you get to do something that you want to do."

Every morning your prospect will be thinking of you as he sees how slowly those jellybeans disappear.

#20. Get your prospect to recruit immediately.

One network marketer has no problem getting his new prospects to make appointments.

How does he do it?

First, he gives a complete presentation to his prospect. When the prospect says that he wants to join, my friend says this:

"The only way that you can join with me is to first set appointments for your first two presentations. If you can't set these two appointments, well, I don't think this business is for you."

What does his prospect do?

His prospect immediately gets on the telephone and sets appointments for two presentations. His prospect is already working the business before he has even joined the business!

#21. Use a "grabber."

What is a grabber?

It is something unique or different that will get your prospect's attention. For example, if you sell beachfront property, you could have a small bag of sand stapled to your sales letter to grab your prospect's attention. The small bag of sand is a sample of what you are selling.

If you sold healthy products, attach a bag of herbal tea to your sales letter or business card,

A pre-paid gift card, a two-dollar bill, or anything different that ties in with your product or opportunity could be a grabber. Don't limit your grabbers to just sales letters. Use them with business cards, brochures, and your person-to-person encounters. Just use your imagination.

Want some more grabber ideas?

Instead of giving a prospect a business card, why not write a $1 check to your prospect. Your personal check has your name, address and telephone number and your prospect will be sure not to throw the check away.

Instead of just sending a letter, why not attach a new lottery ticket to the letter? You can tell the prospect that if the lottery ticket is not a winner, then the prospect can still win by taking advantage of your opportunity. People get excited about lottery tickets.

Instead of a corporate brochure, hand your prospect a snapshot of someone enjoying your product. Or how about a picture of you enjoying a vacation purchased with last month's bonus check? Pictures are hard for people to throw away.

Get the idea?

Use a grabber to get your prospect's attention and interest. You can't prospect uninterested people.

#22. How to meet people at parties.

If you are not a naturally outgoing party person, how are you going to approach strangers to start a conversation? Rachel Rogers of England gave me this tip on how to meet people at parties.

"When you arrive at the party, immediately go to the kitchen. Pick up a tray of nibbles (appetizers), then go to each guest and offer them a nibble. This gives you an excuse to meet new people that is not so artificial. You will have a chance to meet everyone at the party."

Want more prospects? Go to more parties.

The key is your conversation.

Here is your chance to be with prospects who want to change their lives. Maybe in your conversation you could create interested prospects by saying things such as:

* "So what are you going to do next year so it will be better than this year?"

* "Are you okay with going to work six days a week again for another year?"

* "Do you think you could be a better boss than your current boss?"

* "Hmmm, another year ... fifty weeks for the company, two weeks for us."

* "Figure you will get a huge raise next year?"

* "So how many more years to retirement before you will have some free time?"

Parties sound like fun now, don't they?

Network marketing is easy when we know what to say and do.

#23. Start your own association.

People love associations. They join associations. They participate in associations.

Non-profit or minimal profit associations don't threaten prospects. Association members love to recruit and promote the association to others.

So instead of trying to retail vitamins to senior citizens, why not start the Nutrition For Elders Association? You could have monthly meetings with guest speakers on health. You would create a great prospecting list from the association roster, but it gets better. You are the association founder. You have the respect of the members. It would be easy to recommend vitamins to the members.

Why not start the World Traveler Association? It would be much easier than selling travel packages directly to cold prospects. Your local group could have monthly meetings and social events. As the association founder, you would have many trusted members coming to you.

Why not start the Hometown Entrepreneur Association? Your monthly meetings could have guest speakers such as tax and bookkeeping professionals, bankers talking about checking account features, and of course ... you. You could talk about low-cost business start-ups and networking. They will at least listen to you. You are the founder.

Why not start the Hometown Salesmen Association? Here salesmen can get together for a monthly meal and swap stories on how hard it is to make a living in their jobs. Everyone pays for his or her own meal and the restaurant gives <u>you</u> your meal for free. After all, you brought the restaurant all this extra business.

It is easy to find prospects when there is a room full of salesmen complaining about their jobs.

Why not start the Hometown Managers Association? To be a member, you must have a management job. Members could be a personnel manager from the bank, an assistant manager at a local fast-food restaurant, or a bored middle management employee from the local manufacturing plant. Do managers ever wish they could be their own boss? Certainly! They get tired of working long, stressful hours to help someone else make a lot of money.

Get the idea? You can have an informal association of housewives, beer drinkers, engineers, restaurant workers, government workers, fans for the local sports team, Mustang owners, and weekend joggers.

The key is: You must be the association founder.

This makes it easy for you to make contacts and appointments with the association members.

#24. How to get people to ask you for a prospecting tool.

I had lunch with Gerry Vannoy. He told me how he tripled the number of prospects who **asked him** for a prospecting tool. Here is what he does.

Gerry uses a generic prospecting book with an attractive cover that offers a great benefit. He used to place the book on his table when eating at a restaurant. He noticed that prospects from other tables would look at the book, but would never approach him.

So Gerry started putting **two** books on the table. Now the prospects started to come to him and asked him if they could see a copy of the book.

It seems if there is only **one** book, prospects are hesitant to ask. If there are two books, prospects feel comfortable about approaching you and asking about the book.

Why not try this with your best educational prospecting tool? Make it easy for prospects to feel comfortable about approaching you.

#25. Let a charity find you fresh leads.

Whether it is a relative or the neighbor's kid, we all get talked into the $5 charity candy bar sale. We buy some candy bars out of obligation to the charity; but then sometimes, we just love chocolate delivered to our door.

We don't want most charity fund-raising products, but we buy out of guilt and we do want to help.

But what if we offered a product or service that people wanted? That makes it even easier for the club or organization to raise money.

What can you offer to get an appointment with the person in charge of fundraising?

How about offering to give 100% of your profit to the organization? It is pretty hard for the person in charge to say "No" to an appointment request with that offer.

Why give 100% of your profit away to the organization?

1. They will find new customers for your product or service. Some of these customers will love your product or service, and may become distributors. This is free advertising for you.

2. Your sales volume will go up and you might even qualify for more bonuses from your company.

3. Some of your new customers might tell their friends about your product or service. These referrals are gold. What a great way to spread the word about what you do.

This is sounding so good that you might even want to give more than 100% of your profits!

Why the club or organization will love you.

1. Many clubs and organizations do their fundraising once or twice a year. You don't have to interfere with their present campaigns. Your campaign can be "extra" revenue for them to help fill in their funding gaps. Depending on your product or service, you might be able to provide a monthly income as an ongoing campaign.

2. The fundraising committees have to get volunteers to coordinate everything. If you offer to do most of the coordination for them, you will be a hero.

Great prospects for fundraising locations?

Supermarkets and large warehouse clubs are always looking to give back to the community. Many of them will welcome another chance to show the community that they care.

Look for places where fundraising occurs already. Do you see someone selling Girl Scout cookies outside a store? An animal shelter charity with a table with brochures? These locations are pre-sold on giving you free space to raise money for a good cause.

Be ready to adjust.

1. You will have to adjust to the time slots available at your chosen location.

2. A low-cost product or service will work best. It is easy to make a small donation on impulse, and your product or service will feel like a bonus to the prospect.

3. Make sure your product or service doesn't compete with your chosen location. That's just common sense.

4. Set up your table or booth not only for sales, but also for collecting leads. Not everyone has money left when they leave the store, and some people may not be interested now, but they could be interested later.

5. Set up your table or booth for a fast-moving audience. People will quickly stream by you and your offer.

6. Raffles work. It is easier to collect names and contact information if it is on an entry to a drawing. Is there a prize, gift, or sample that you could give everyone who enters?

7. Allow people to donate directly to the charity, without purchasing your product or service.

8. Your lead capture entry form might pre-sell or pre-sort your prospects with verbiage such as:

"Check here to receive the special report, _____, via email."

"Check here to schedule a free _____."

9. Remember that your space is free because you are raising funds. Don't forget to take good care of the club or organization. Make them #1 in your decisions.

10. Be in charge of the selling if you can. Charities are not good at selling products or services for someone else. Their volunteers just assume the other volunteers will do it.

Start small.

To build trust, you could start with a mini-fundraising campaign. It could be as simple as:

* A featured article in their newsletter describing and offering your products and services.

* A fundraising letter they send out to their supporters.

* A social media campaign where they ask their supporters to put your carefully-written message on their Facebook pages.

* A speech by you at one of their meetings where you make an offer.

* A free booth they give you at their big yearly event.

Supporters will buy more and ask fewer questions if most or all of your profits go to the fundraiser.

Supporters get a good product or service, the organization or club gets more funds, and you get customers and prospects. A win-win-win promotion.

#26. Cruel and unusual punishment.

Of course we can't find **all** of the prospects in our organization ourselves. We need our new distributors to find prospects **also**.

While traveling with Rasmus Skovmand in Denmark, he discussed the best way to get distributors off to a fast start.

His conclusion?

To motivate your distributors, do this:

Take their television remote home with you. Let them know they can get their remote back after they have sponsored their first four distributors, or after they have acquired their first four customers.

When your new distributors look at a television that doesn't turn on, they will think about promoting their business.

#27. Use gift certificates to lock in prospects.

Two great reasons to use gift certificates in your business:

1. Not only will prospects and customers use them personally, they can also give the certificates to others. This expands your market beyond your personal contacts. It is like having other people do the prospecting for you.

2. If your prospect has a gift certificate or discount coupon, he won't want to pay full price to a competitor. You can expect a call from a hot, motivated spender.

Some examples of gift certificates or coupons that you could create.

Use your imagination. Consider this an advertising expense to get a long-term customer or distributor. Here are some ideas:

* $20 off your first cellphone bill.

* Free bottle of minerals when you buy one bottle of vitamins.

* Free dinner for two includes miracle diet samples and video.

* Lipstick and full facial for only $1.

* Free car wash while attending our 30-minute business briefing.

* Free babysitting while attending our Saturday business training.

* Free facial with your body wrap order.

This gift certificate idea gets even better.

Have customers **pay** you and still network for you.

A customer buys a gift certificate from you to give to a friend as a gift. The friend becomes your new customer. Now your customers are actually prospecting and networking for you.

So do anything you can to get a gift certificate into your customers' hands.

Maybe you have to discount your product or service, or even give an extra bonus or gift to induce your customer to purchase the gift certificate. Maybe you have to pay $10 out of your pocket to make the gift certificate a great value. So what?

Your investment is an inexpensive way to prospect. Much cheaper than advertising.

#28. Free dinner premium to get a new product user.

If you are on a tight budget, try this idea.

Find a restaurant owner with children. Offer to pay a babysitter for two hours in exchange for a certificate for two dinners. The restaurant owners will love the offer, as the dinners will only cost them a small percentage of the retail value.

Then take the dinner certificates and offer them to a new prospect for becoming a first-time customer of your products. For example, if your product costs $30, you will include the dinner certificates as a premium. The customer gets your $30 product PLUS $30 in dinner certificates.

How could a prospect refuse that great offer?

What a great way to expand your product user base. Happy product users are easy to convert into brand-new distributors for your business.

#29. Catching fish in a fishbowl.

Can you tell your future by looking into a crystal ball? Maybe not. However, you can create a great prospecting future by looking into a fish bowl.

Many of our readers have used this technique from *Start SuperNetworking* to find members for their personal networking groups. But did you know you can use this method to find prospects for your business too?

Local restaurants often promote their business by offering a drawing for a free lunch. Business people place their business cards in a fishbowl, hoping for a free meal.

After the big prize drawing (the free lunch), the business cards in the fish bowl are dumped in the trashcan so that next month's drawing can begin.

Want prospects with real business experience? No problem.

Find several restaurants in your area catering to the business lunch crowd and start using the "fish bowl" strategy.

Each restaurant attracts different business people from the local area. That means the more restaurants you find, the more potential prospects you can reach.

Ask the manager, "What do you do with those business cards after the drawing?"

You will hear, "I just throw the old business cards in the trash."

You can then say, "Let me take those old business cards off your hands!"

Prepare to leave with stacks of business cards of experienced business people who could be your next best prospects.

What is on a business card? Name, company, business address, and daytime phone number. Sometimes even a home phone number. And usually there is at least a hint of their occupation.

But what do you know about these people who left their business cards?

For starters, they all have jobs that interfere with their week. They would likely prefer to be doing something else with their time. Maybe they could be fishing, spending time with their children, shopping, traveling, or having more interesting hobbies. But we do know this ... Their job is taking up too much of their time!

Are these people overpaid or underpaid? If you took a survey, they would all say the boss pays them much less than they are worth.

Do these people love working hard so the boss gets a big house for his retirement? Or would they rather be working to build their own retirement accounts?

Do these people love waking up early in the morning, leaving their families, and commuting to and from work? No. They would love to wake up when they were "tired of sleeping" and commute from the bedroom to the living room.

Yes, you know a lot about these people. They want a better life. Someone needs to give them an option. That could be you.

How can you approach these people without getting the restaurant in trouble? Try a short note like this:

*****

You FINALLY Won!

Dear _____ ,

Remember dropping off your business card to get a free lunch?

Well, I'm sorry to say you didn't get the free lunch this week, but you did win! You won the second prize sponsored by my company!

Just for being adventurous enough to leave your business card, here is your coupon for a free (your premium), with a retail value of ($).

This _____ will:

* Benefit 1 (use the top three benefits of your offer)

* Benefit 2

* Benefit 3

Call me at XXX-XXX-XXXX to redeem your coupon in five days, and I will treat you to a dessert myself!

Sincerely,

Joe Networker

*****

What are you giving them for second prize?

* Maybe it is your recruiting audio, *How To Start Your Own Mega-Business For Micro-Dollars.*

* Maybe it is your company's latest health product audio with a discount coupon.

* Maybe it is a special report that you call *Personal Entrepreneurial Briefing.*

* Maybe it is a seven-day sample of your hottest product.

The prize is designed to tell you if the person has a spark of interest in what you have to offer.

Since people are too busy to claim small prizes of this nature, only the most interested prospects will call to claim their prize. And when you get that interested prospect to call, make sure to repeat your offer of a free dessert if you meet them face-to-face. It is always better to meet the prospect in person.

This technique will help you get lunchtime appointments with business people. Your evenings will still be free for more presentations.

Want to contact the same prospects again?

Easy. At the end of your first email, say, "By the way, you are automatically entered in next week's contest." Now they will be looking forward to your next email. And who knows? Maybe next week their circumstances change and your email arrives on the perfect day, and at the perfect time, for this prospect.

But the restaurants in my area don't have a fishbowl that collects business cards.

No problem. Create your own campaign. And since it is your campaign, you can be more selective in how you attract new prospects.

Think about the prospects you want to talk to. What if they had these four qualifications?

1. The prospects are local. If someone leaves their business card at the local restaurant, chances are they live or work locally. Local prospects are easier to talk to and to train. You can have them attend your local meeting with prospects. They can come to your local training workshops. And, you can meet and coach them over a cup of coffee. This is a completely different relationship than only talking to someone over the telephone.

2. The prospects have a job or a small business. They have money to spend on getting started, for samples, for products, and for promotions. People with jobs have friends and co-workers, a perfect built-in warm market to contact when they join.

3. They hate their jobs and want to do something else in their lives. Since they hate where they are right now, they may be more open-minded about an opportunity with your business. Dissatisfaction is the motivator for change.

4. They even told us why they hated their jobs!

Where can you find these prospects?

Well, we could go to a large office building and go desk-to-desk talking to the dissatisfied employees. However, security would throw us out.

So again, we will use a fishbowl. But, we will do a little pre-sorting of these prospects and not ask for their business cards. Instead, we will ask them to fill in a little form for a drawing for a free lunch.

First, we get the restaurant owner to allow us to place a fishbowl near their cash register. Think about the location. Wouldn't it be great if the restaurant or sandwich shop was in or near a huge office building or factory? Every day the employees get a 45-minute or one-hour break to leave their jobs to get a bite to eat. You can offer to give away a free lunch. That is less expensive than a dinner. Again, if we want to get good prospects, we have to go where the prospects are.

To the restaurant or sandwich shop owner we would say, "Would it be okay if I give away some free meals?" The owner can say, "Sure, you can give away all the free meals you want to, but only if you pay for those meals." Well, that seems fair.

Will every restaurant allow you to do this? No. But some will.

What will you put on the fishbowl so prospects notice? You could say:

"Win a FREE lunch!"

That is pretty simple. Use your imagination though. Maybe you could make the sign on the fishbowl tie in with your business or product.

What does your entry form look like? First, make it simple. People are in a hurry, so just ask for some basic information, and make sure the information is not too personal. For example, if you ask for telephone numbers, they may be afraid to enter your drawing for a free meal. They fear harassment by pushy salesmen over the telephone.

While it is up to you to decide the basic information you want to collect, here is the minimum you will need:

A. Their first name. That's it. So if you send them an email that they won the free meal, at least it can look personal.

B. An email address. Tell them you need their email address so that you can notify them if they won the free meal.

C. Ask them to fill in the following sentence: "The top reasons I dislike my job are ..."

That's it!

Now you collect your own prospects from the restaurant, and give away that free meal you promised.

By asking the prospects to fill out "why" they hate their job on your entry form, you now have valuable information on how you can serve that prospect better. You already know what motivates them.

And like the earlier example in this chapter, you can award the winner the free meal, and notify everyone else that they won the "second prize" in your drawing.

Will this work everywhere?

Of course not. But, it will work sometimes even if you mess it up.

One lady sent us an email describing her experience with this technique. She placed her fishbowl in a pizza place, not a good location for daytime workers. She also asked for their phone numbers.

Even though she didn't follow the instructions, she still got customers and distributors.

Use your imagination!

#30. Think global - work local.

Barb Pitcock gave me her strategy for people who use leads. She advises distributors to get leads that are local. Many lead companies and providers of Internet leads can sort their leads by area.

If the leads are local, it is easier to telephone them and build a relationship. Why fly 1,000 miles to meet a good lead when you can meet them locally over a cup of coffee?

Speaking of Internet leads, I once heard an Internet professional say that the first thing you should do with an Internet lead is to get them off the Internet. Contact them quickly by telephone to distinguish yourself from all the emails they get daily.

Remember, there is a hierarchy in communication:

Level One: Email (lowest.) A one-way communication.

Level Two: Video, website, audio (better.) Still a one-way communication.

Level Three: Telephone (much better.) Two-way communication. You can hear the tone of their voice too.

Level Four: Video telephone or Skype (see and hear.) Two-way communication. You can see when they roll their eyes.

Level Five: In person (nearly the best.) It's harder to be impolite to someone in person.

Level Six: In person over food (truly the best bonding experience.)

At what level do you communicate?

Always attempt to communicate at the highest level that is available to you. And if you see a prospect who is slightly overweight, just think to yourself:

"Hey, he could be a good networker. He would love to meet prospects over food!"

#31. Choose your seat.

Want to sit with even more prospects?

When flying, try not to get a window seat or an aisle seat. Instead, ask for the middle seat. This way you will have a prospect on either side of you.

How do you get your prospects' email addresses? Easy. Somewhere in the conversation, offer to email them valuable information they may want. For example,

* A travel site that searches for low fares.

* A site with travel tips.

* A recipe.

* Some travel jokes.

Mention that you don't have the information with you, but will email them the information or website address. Then, use a creative signature file to send the prospect to your sales information.

And this isn't just for flying!

At any live event, select your seat wisely. Sit where you can comfortably meet the most people.

#32. Real estate agents.

Let the real estate agent send pre-sold prospects to you.

Stop by your local residential real estate office. There are always lonely salesmen waiting to get a phone call from one of their advertisements.

Sit down and spend a few minutes with one of the bored salesmen and build a little rapport. Ask a question or two about the business, how he finds prospects, etc.

Then, ask the salesman, "How much commission do you earn on people who can't afford to buy the house they want?"

He will reply, "Nothing. If they can't qualify for the bank loan, then there is no sale."

Then, try this proposal. Say, "I have a plan. Now, maybe this won't help the buyer qualify for a house today, but it might put them in position to qualify in a few months. Would that be okay?"

The salesman will usually say, "Sure. That would be okay. A sale in a few months is better than no sale at all. So what is this plan?"

Here is what you can tell the salesman.

"Let's say that your buyer doesn't have enough income to qualify for the monthly payments, or not enough money for the down payment, or needs a few more dollars every month to clear up some past credit problems. If this is the case, you can say this to your buyer:

"'I have a friend named (use your name here.) He is a pretty good guy. You would like him. He helps people earn some extra money each month by starting their own part-time business. This might give you enough extra money to qualify for the house of your dreams. Here is his telephone number. Give him a call. He is a busy guy, but you will enjoy talking with him. I will make sure to give him your telephone number the next time we are together, just in case you were not able to reach him.'"

What happens next?

You could get a pre-sold prospect for your network marketing business. The real estate agent might make a sale to this prospect in a few months when the prospect starts earning more money. This is a win-win situation.

When the prospect calls you, the conversation might go something like this:

Prospect: "Hello, is this (your name)?"

You: "Yes."

Prospect: "The local real estate agent told me to call you. He says that you help people start a part-time business and earn some extra money. Is that right?"

You: "Yes."

Prospect: "Sounds great. Could we get together sometime and talk?"

You: "Yes."

Prospect: "I have a full-time job, but I do have weekends free. Can we get together for a cup of coffee on Saturday morning?"

You: "Yes."

Prospect: "Great. Let's meet at the Hot Cup Cafe on Maple Street at 9:00am. Is that okay for you?"

You: "Yes."

Now, you don't have to have great phone skills when pre-sold prospects are begging you for an appointment. You now have quality prospects coming to you.

The real estate agent isn't the only person you can help. Just think of all the other professionals who meet quality people who need some extra income.

#33. A subtle prospecting tool.

"Is there a unique prospecting method I can use to stand out from the crowd?"

Try using your personal newsletter instead of a video, audio, or brochure. Why?

Videos, audios, and brochures are commercials for your business.

Your prospect reads or listens with sales resistance.

If your prospect receives a copy of your newsletter, it is not perceived as a commercial. Instead, the prospect feels that he is peeking inside your business. He can see:

* How your business is doing.

* How other people you sponsored are doing.

* Great product or service testimonials.

* A positive news article that relates to your product.

* Who the top producers are.

* New announcements from your company.

* How your newest member paid for his Christmas holiday with cash.

* Personal stories about why people joined your opportunity.

* Details about the free company trip.

* How John and Mary quit their jobs and now are at home with their children.

Since your newsletter is not a commercial, you will get your prospect's unbiased attention. So try sending your newsletter to your prospect list on a regular basis. Who knows? Maybe your newsletter will arrive on the day that your prospect decides to make a change in his life.

Do you think this idea will cause you to change how your newsletter looks? Great!

Or maybe this idea will motivate you to write your own newsletter. Great!

Most networkers think that they have to have a large downline before they write their first newsletter. But they are missing the point.

If you use your newsletter as a prospecting tool, you will want to write your own newsletter now.

But I can't write!

Then do an audio or video version. Maybe that is easier for you. Create a quick four-minute update on your business.

It is easy for your prospect to say, "Sure, send me a copy of your newsletter." No pressure. No sales pitch.

But constant exposure to you, your products or services, and your opportunity will accumulate over time. When the time is right for them, your prospects "will see what you see" and want to contact you.

#34. Where to get a list of entrepreneurs who are workers!

In many places, entrepreneurs who start their own business use an "assumed name" such as: AAA Plumbing, Ace Carpet Cleaning, John's Handyman Service, or Top of the World Roofing. Most places require a business using an assumed name to register the name for public records.

Public records? Hmmm, sounds like a great prospecting list, doesn't it?

Here we have a list of entrepreneurs who actually act on their dreams. Wow!

But don't act too quickly. Our friend Craig Tucker recommends contacting the entrepreneurs one year after their initial registration. Why?

Because in their first year, the entrepreneurs are excited and focused on their new business. But after one year, reality sets in. They see the problems of payroll, licenses, permits, long hours, bookkeeping, etc.

They still have an entrepreneurial dream, but they want a simpler solution.

Network marketing is simple and less risky than most traditional businesses.

Remember, most people are quitters.

You might think, "Well, what if other people get the same list from the public records? I want to talk to fresh people who others haven't approached."

No worries.

It takes time and effort to follow up with any list of people. Most people give up after a few calls. They start with the names that begin with letter "A" and maybe even get through a few more letters of the alphabet. And then, they quit.

So if you want to talk to fresher leads, untouched by low-energy quitters, do this.

When you get your list of leads, start at the bottom! Start with the letter "Z." Most quitters never get this far and the leads are virtually untouched.

#35. Think outside the box.

One ultra-innovative distributor wanted to run a local online ad. Unfortunately, the website would not allow business opportunity ads.

So, she came up with another plan to attract prospects. She would not let problems like this get in her way.

Here was her solution.

She posted her ad in the "Women Looking For Men" section of the website. This is what the ad said:

*****

**Wanted: a man who was once successful,
lost everything and is starting over!**

What was that? Unemployed or soon to be, you say? Lost everything? Fine with me!

I know you have drive and passion, but things happen. I launched another company four years ago and it's growing like crazy and I can't handle it alone. I need a man.

Truth is, men do better in my industry. I was thinking it would be nice if I could find a man that wants to rebuild his own life and we can work together. I love cash flow like everyone else and am willing to work for it.

I am interested in entrepreneurs or business executives. I'm not here to rescue anyone - I'm here to launch you back into greatness and have fun along the way!! Email me if interested in knowing more.

*****

She posted her ad at midnight.

She had 300 responses by noon, just 12 hours later.

There were plenty of strange responses that she sorted out quickly, but she sponsored almost 10% of the qualified responses.

She always presorted via social media and met the prospects in public places.

Don't let obstacles stop you.

This lady could have given up and not advertised for new prospects. Instead, she created a solution to her problem. And just think, how many relationship sites are on the Internet that she could use?

This lady could have chosen to give up when people told her, "Advertising on the Internet doesn't work." But what these negative people are saying is, "<u>Our</u> advertising on the Internet doesn't work."

A little bit of creativity and skill can separate us from the crowd.

#36. How to stand out from your competition.

If you sell diet products, offer to buy your customer lunch at a local restaurant. (Make sure they have a low-calorie selection.)

If you sell cleaning products, offer to provide your customer a maid for a few hours. (The maid might be happy for a chance to get a new client.)

If you sell skincare products, offer your customer a free appointment at a local hairdresser. (The hairdresser might be happy for a chance to get a new customer.)

If you sell travel services, bring your prospect to a frequent-travelers' party as your guest.

Get the picture? Invest a little in your original customer. Why?

1. It is easier to keep a new customer when you offer a terrific deal.

2. You get a chance for repeat business from this satisfied customer.

3. It is easier to recruit distributors from satisfied customers than from cold prospects.

#37. Become a walking billboard.

Okay, this might be a little over-the-top. If your "gear" stands out, looks different, is out of the ordinary or attracts attention, well, what could be more fun than having prospects coming to you and asking you about your business?

Imagine you see someone in a football jersey from your local team. You won't even notice that person as he walks by. But, if you see someone at the game in the opposing team's apparel, you will definitely notice that person.

And, if you see someone in a football jersey from another team, with his face painted, wearing a full wig, and sporting shoulder pads, you really notice. Different gets attention!

You silently ask yourself questions such as:

* Is this person sane?

* Why is he at this game?

* Why is he such a superfan of his team?

Sometimes our curiosity gets the best of us and we just have to start asking that person some questions. Conversation has started!

How does this work in our business?

One of the biggest networking companies grew with the simplicity of people wearing a button. It made people ask questions and start a conversation. Prospects came to them.

Do you have access to a shirt that creates a conversation? If your company doesn't offer one, can you find a generic shirt that creates conversations?

Will everyone magically ask about your shirt? No, only the people who are interested. New distributors find it much easier when people are asking them for more information.

What if you can't find a great shirt?

Then create your own shirt or "gear" that will start conversations. You can customize, screen, and embroider almost anything. Think beyond a shirt. Consider:

* Hats.

* Jackets.

* Scarves.

* Giant buttons.

* Gloves.

* Purses.

* Briefcases.

* Giant business cards.

Giant business cards?

Why not make your business cards into the size of a greeting card? People will definitely notice your card.

If you decide to use a regular-sized business card, purchase some self-laminating card holders at your local office supply store. Punch a hole and attach it to a lanyard. You've found a quick and inexpensive way to wear your card.

Not a fan of wearing your business card around your neck? Strap the lanyard around your purse strap, your computer backpack, side bag, anything you use on a regular basis.

You have to get out and about almost every day anyway. You might as well get some free advertising while you are completing your routine errands.

Advertise on your vehicle.

A window decal or car sign advertises your website or telephone number. Usually a telephone number works best. Your window decal or car sign should have a four- or five-word headline or reason to contact you now.

Your message has to be short. Really short. If your message is too long, the words get too small to read and can't be read quickly.

Focus on just one product or one benefit for that product to make the message short.

For example, if you sold diet cookies, your message would say,

"Eat cookies - lose weight!"

If you sold skincare products,

"Instant wrinkle remover!"

If you were looking for prospects to join your business,

"Great part-time job!" or "Fire your boss!" or "Five-day weekends!"

So work hard on simplifying and focusing your message to one sales point only.

Now, back to your car. Just think of how many cars will see your message every day. It is a one-time investment with no ongoing costs. Window decals are cheap, but if you see that it works, consider a whole wrap for your car. Now you have plenty of space to advertise. Some distributors report getting back their car wrap investment in new business in just a few months.

If your car attracted more prospects to you daily, where would you drive? Where would you park? In the commuter parking lot? By the health club?

But why not go a step further to increase your exposure? Think of how many more prospects you would get if your mom, your friends, and your pizza delivery man would put your decal on the back of their cars too!

How to stand out in an overcrowded environment.

A Chicago restaurant gave away 1,000 coffee mugs with its name imprinted on them. The cost? Less than $1,500.

Great advertising ... and it was cheap advertising. Every day up to 1,000 potential customers would see the restaurant's advertising while they drank their morning coffee. Maybe their potential customers would think:

"Hmmm. Wonder where my spouse and I could go to dinner tonight?"

Since many restaurants have a food cost of about 33%, let's do the math. The restaurant would have to sell about $2,250 in food to break even. That's about 200 meals or only 100 couples visiting the restaurant just one time.

The reality? More than 100 couples came into the restaurant. Often they would bring their friends. And many of the couples became regular customers.

Yes. The money kept flowing in.

But what does this have to do with my long-time friend, Dave Feldman? Well, I received a package in the mail. Guess what was in the package?

A coffee mug with a picture of Dave and me. Below our picture it says:

**Big Al and Dave
MLM Friends Forever**

So out goes the restaurant mug and now I use the mug with our picture. And I think of Dave daily.

Sneaky, but effective marketing.

Everyone uses mugs. Some people drink coffee or hot chocolate and other people use the mugs to store pencils or grow a small plant. All of these mugs could have your special message or picture.

What can you put on your special mugs?

You could advertise your opportunity, products or services. Imagine the following messages imprinted on your mugs along with your telephone number:

* Why not be your own boss?

* Get cheap long-distance rates!

* Time for a career change?

* Am I paid what I am worth?

* Next time, I will schedule my own vacation.

* Beautiful, younger-looking skin in just 17 seconds.

Or you can get more creative.

* Thanks for helping me with my business. (Add your picture.)

* Tired of commuting? (Put this on a no-spill travel mug your prospects can use in their cars.)

* Lose weight while you drink. (Maybe you sell thermogenic coffee or weight-loss tea.)

You could put your entire compensation plan on the side of a giant latte mug. Prospects love those really big mugs they used in the popular TV show, *Friends*. Those 15-ounce mugs are massive.

You want to promote your business inexpensively by creatively getting your name, products, services and opportunity in front of qualified prospects.

Why fight with competitors by spending big bucks on display ads, email lists, social media ads, etc. when you can have **all** of your prospect's attention? You don't have to fight on a crowded playing field. Create your own exclusive playing field.

So don't just think coffee mugs.

Think:

"Where else can I have my prospect's total attention?"

Here are some ideas for your promotional ads to get you started:

* Antenna balls

* Backpacks for kids

* Balloons

* Beer mugs

* Beverage can holders

* Beverage coolers

* Bumper stickers

* Calculators

* Calendars

* Caps

* Decals

* First-aid kits

* Flags

* Flashlights

* Floor mats

* Ice scrapers

* Key rings

* Luggage tags

* Magnetic signs

* Memo pad cubes

* Mouse pads

* Paper or plastic bags

* Paperweights

* Pens and pencils

* Personalized stationery

* Pill boxes

* Placemats

* Playing cards

* Puzzles

* Refrigerator magnets

* Seat cushions

* Shirts

* Towels

* Umbrellas

* Watches

* Water bottles

This promotional technique is easy. All you have to do is ask yourself this question:

"Where can I get my prospect's complete attention?"

Then, fine-tune your headline or message to attract favorable attention to your offer.

Just remember to keep your message short. Not much room for a long headline on a key chain!

#38. How to use a "bird dog" without being a hunter.

"Bird dogs" are not just for hunters. Salespeople use them all the time. Why can't you?

Here is how one entrepreneur, Joe, turned every prospect into a prospecting machine for his business. Like every other car salesman, he had a standard business card. On the front of the card, he had his contact information plus this message:

$100 For Every New Car You Help Me Sell!

On the back of the card, he had this offer for his "bird dog":

Dear Joe, please treat my friend _____ right!

And if you make the sale, treat me right!

Name _____

Phone _____

Even if you never purchased a car from Joe, he put you to work. When you walked away with a stack of his business cards in your hand, you left thinking, "Maybe I should buy my car from someone who is willing to pay me money." Or you thought, "Wow. I can get $100 if I find someone who is thinking about a car. I bet I have a couple of friends who might qualify right now."

Could you do this in your business?

This works very well in network marketing because not everyone wants to build a group or even use your products. However, they wouldn't mind making some extra money referring hot prospects to you. We know distributors who quickly added hundreds of dollars to their incomes just from these kinds of referrals.

These "bird dogs" think of you when someone mentions your product line or starting a new business, and they tell their contacts to give you a call. It doesn't happen every day. But sooner or later, someone in your pack of "bird dogs" will hear something to "jog" his memory. If enough of your bird dogs are out there "hunting," you could be getting new business every week or every day from this network.

The beauty of the "bird dog" system in networking is that you only pay out the bonus on the first sale. Most of your new customers will end up buying from you again and again.

How could you use this technique to your advantage?

Have the back of your business card remind people about the reward for referring people to your business. Make it the last thing you tell people when you finish an "unsuccessful" prospecting meeting.

To the uninterested prospect, you could say, "Mary, I know you don't want to do the business right now, but I want to tell you how you can still make some money. It is right here on the back of my business card. How many of these business cards can I give you? Is five okay?"

Or at the end of a telephone call with an uninterested prospect, you could say, "Mary, I know you don't want to do the business right now, but I want to tell you how you can still make some money. It is right here on the back of my business card. How many of these business cards can I send you?"

What could you offer?

Here are some ideas.

* You could offer $25 cash for each new business-builder someone refers. Make sure there are some criteria this business-builder meets before spending your money. You should establish a minimum target, such as buying a distributor kit and purchasing $100 in product. Or, you might require the business-builder to be on the monthly auto-ship program.

* Let's say a customer referred you to a new customer. You could offer to pay next month's order for your referring customer. It might be worth it to have a new, long-term customer.

* Buy dinner for anyone who refers you to a prospect who joins your business. If you end up buying lots of dinners at the local restaurant, possibly the restaurant owner will want to join, or at least help you find even more referrals.

* Remember, your finder's fee for your "bird dog" doesn't have to be cash.

The average person knows about 200 people.

Think of it this way. You don't want to talk to the 200 people your customer or friend knows. You only want to talk to the five or ten that have the right timing and interest. That is why "bird dogs" are great. They can point you to just the right people at the right time.

#39. Captive audiences.

How to fill up your room with smiling prospects.

An enterprising pizza restaurant owner might make this offer:

"If you have an 'A' on your report card, come in for free pizza this Tuesday night. Just bring your parents."

Why would the restaurant make this offer? Because they make plenty of profit on the food and drinks the parents order.

Could you make the same offer?

Could you partner with your local pizza restaurant?

You would have a captive audience of parents. Why not make a short presentation or give out information about your business? After all, you are the co-sponsor.

And while you have the whole family in the room, explain how a part-time income from your business would pay for the whole family to take their next holiday at Disney World! Get the children involved with pressuring their parents to earn a little bit more so they can have the holiday of their dreams.

But what if it costs me $10 per person?

Maybe your local pizza restaurant owner is not open-minded, and you have to pay $10 for every parent who comes on Tuesday night. This cost is still a lot less than buying leads. Let's say that you purchase leads at $5 each, and it takes you 10 leads to get a presentation. This means that you have spent $50 just to get in front of one "live" prospect to give a presentation.

If you drive across town to meet a prospect for a cup of coffee, it will probably cost you $10 in car expenses, the cost of your coffee, the cost of finding that prospect, and quite a bit of your time - just to get in front of one "live" prospect to give a presentation.

See a trend?

It costs money and time to get in front of prospects.

So why not bribe prospects instead?

For less than you are spending now to get in front of prospects, you could actually buy your next-door neighbor lunch if he agrees to listen to your presentation.

You might say: "But how do I know that my next-door neighbor will be a highly-qualified, motivated prospect?"

Well, there is no guarantee. But then again, there is no guarantee that the lead you prospected will be highly-qualified and motivated either.

The point is: Look at your costs to get in front of qualified prospects.

#40. Immerse your prospects.

In the 1990s, the "slow food experience" was popular in Slovenia and parts of Italy. What was the slow food experience?

The restaurant issues a private invitation to customers. The restaurant closes to the public for six to eight hours for the event. The chef explains and demonstrates how he prepares certain dishes and invites the customers to try each one. Only small amounts are served as 20 or 30 different dishes are created and sampled over the six or eight hours. Of course, plenty of wine is also served.

The customers pay about $50 for the "slow food experience" of eating for the next several hours. The customers enjoy meeting the chef and tasting new creations, and love the social atmosphere of the occasion.

How can you use this idea in your business?

Try the following:

Let's say you sell diet products. Charge $50 for a body-shaping afternoon. The afternoon includes an aerobics class with personal instruction, a dance class, a cooking class, and a diet lecture.

The money you receive is **profit** as the health club provides the instructors and a room to help promote their club, and you can get a cookware representative to do the cooking demonstration. Now you have a captive audience. You targeted your exact audience (they want to re-shape their bodies) and you educated your audience during the afternoon activities.

You simply take orders for diet products at the end of the afternoon.

If you sell skincare products, what can you do?

You can arrange for a "Change Your Image" afternoon for only $40.

First, you get students from a local beauty school to do your participants' nails and hair. They need the practice and the cost would be minimal.

Next, provide a speaker for a makeover and color-analysis session. For a few dollars more, you can arrange for a couple of babysitters on-site.

Finally, provide some food. Maybe you can get a person who sells diet products to whip up some tasty shakes and a vegetable tray.

This all-afternoon session will cost much less than a single visit to a beauty salon.

You now have a captive audience for your skincare products.

When word gets out about your successful event, you will easily pre-sell tickets for your next event. Standing room only!

Or, if you don't have the contacts to pre-sell tickets, have other professionals buy tickets that they can give to their customers as bonuses. An expensive dress shop could give away a ticket with every overpriced dress. Or, a health club could give away a ticket as an incentive to try a 60-day membership.

"How To Retire Early" seminar.

Invite people to spend a Saturday afternoon with:

* The real estate agent who shows people how to invest in local real estate.

* The insurance agent who shows how to save money on insurance.

* The stockbroker who will talk about long-term investing.

* The budget counselor who helps people pay off their debt faster.

The attendees will need more money to invest and reduce their current debt. So why don't you be the final speaker who shows the attendees how to create a part-time income with your business? You will be adding one more option to their lives.

These prospects want more, and are willing to do something about it. They invested a Saturday afternoon. They are serious prospects.

#41. Secret ad kept my phone ringing all day.

One network marketing team built an entire campaign around "Energy Drink Testers Wanted." The company introduced a packet of drink mixes that competed with other energy drinks in the marketplace.

Rather than randomly pass out individual serving packets of the energy drink powder, the team decided to attract new and eager prospects for potential customers. This is the ad they ran:

*****

Energy Drink Testers Wanted

Free sample in exchange for your honest opinion!

Call <Distributor's First Name> at: xxx-xxx-xxxx

Or visit xxxxxxx.com for details

*****

This one little ad created an amazing response. An overwhelming response. Who knew it could be so easy? Plus, all of the telephone numbers and email addresses provided were accurate, because the prospects actually **wanted** someone to contact them right away.

One distributor told me, "I have 198 local leads (within two hours of my home) and 39 long-distance leads." Now, that is a lot of prospects!

Another distributor commented, "With this ad, people volunteer and force their address and phone details on you. They can't wait to be a tester."

Now, you know something in your ad is hot when you don't have to beg people to give you their contact details. In this case, the word "tester" was the key to all the excitement. "Tester" means free, and many people love to give their opinions. And who wouldn't want to be first to try a new product? Yes, there is some magic in the word, "tester."

And for the distributors using the Internet, all they did was send their prospects to a simple landing page to register their details. Then, the distributor would call these prospects back as quickly as possible.

Where did the distributors find all these prospects?

1. They put up signs in their local area. Bulletin boards, restaurant windows, grocery stores and community centers.

2. They advertised on local websites.

3. They posted on Facebook and other social media.

4. They put the offer on their business cards.

5. They made coupons for the local merchants to give away.

6. They made the offer to health clubs.

7. They gave coupons and flyers to dental offices, dry cleaners, and restaurants.

8. They even passed out flyers at the commuter train station in the morning to tired, grumpy people going to their jobs.

Getting prospects to respond was easy because they had the right words that attracted interested, motivated prospects!

The good and the bad.

First, the good.

Some distributors complained, "The ad works too well. I stopped advertising because I can't possibly buy enough samples right now."

I bet most advertisers would want that problem.

These distributors ordered their original samples and got those samples into their prospects' hands. Then, from the new orders of their energy drink, they financed their next purchase of samples. They grew as fast as they could with a small budget, but they quickly created enough profits to continue building with an ever-increasing budget.

Now, consider this.

If the ad is working too well, and too many leads are coming in, that would be a great incentive to encourage a prospect to join. You could say, "I either have to sponsor you to help, or I will have to stop running this ad. So please join. I have so many people waiting to talk to you already."

And now for the bad.

Some distributors said their ad didn't work. But when investigating their ads, we found they had **changed** the ad. They changed the wording, or included something about a business opportunity.

This is a great lesson. Don't change what is working. Of course it is okay to test something new, but don't say the campaign is not working because you changed what was working.

The biggest flaw in the changes was this:

Distributors tried to sell the product and the opportunity at the same time.

It is good to choose one or the other. It is too confusing for the new prospect when you present too many choices. Plus, then we come across as a salesman. Prospects recoil and go into protective mode, not willing to try something new or to change.

Keeping the campaign simple with a single choice works best.

How did they follow up with the prospects?

After they tested the energy drink, the distributor asked,

"What did you like best about it?"

Through trial and error, they found that this one question worked the best.

What happened when they asked a different question, such as:

"What do you think?"

The replies from the prospect seemed more negative. The prospects would say,

"I am not sure if I like it or not."

When asked what they liked **best**, prospects started thinking about the best aspects of the sample they tried. The prospects tended to focus on the good aspects, and didn't think about the negatives.

It is important to test different approaches and follow-up phrases. Find the ones that work the best, and then pass those tested phrases on to your downline for duplication.

After the prospect's feedback on the sample, the distributors would ask them if they would like to place an order. If they said "No," the distributors gave the prospects information on how they could order at a later date. If the prospects said "Yes," the distributors took the order.

But what about your product or service?

Maybe you don't sell energy drinks, but you can apply some or all of the above lessons to your business. Want some ideas?

* "Fragrance testers wanted." Do you sell fragrances or essential oils? This could attract interested prospects who love your type of products.

* "Insomniacs only!" Have a product that is a sleeping aid?

* "Must be overweight and impatient!" That would bring prospects who need to lose weight, and are willing to make a quick decision.

* "Only for people who have more than 20 pounds to lose." Now you are targeting a long-term diet customer.

* "Love the environment?" This could attract prospects for natural cleaning products, a product that reduces car emissions, or green energy solutions.

* "Skincare product testers wanted." Does your natural skincare line produce a difference in just a few days? Only prospects who are looking for a change will call. This is important. Some prospects don't want to change from their current skincare products, so you don't want to attract these non-prospects.

Do you see a pattern?

By using some exclusivity in our headlines, we can attract the best prospects and make them feel special. These headlines make prospects feel like we are talking directly to them. And at the same time, we are also sorting out the people who don't want to try something new.

But can I use this to promote my opportunity?

Of course. Maybe you can't give a person a sample of your opportunity, but you can use the same headline sorting techniques to find prospects who are looking for exactly what you have to offer.

Instead of giving them a sample, you could give these prospects an audio, a book, or a website link. These types of tools are only a one-way communication though. They just talk **at** people. If you are brand-new, this is your only option until you learn how to talk to prospects effectively.

If you have mastered some skills on how to present your opportunity, with tested and proven words, then it is much, much better to have a one-on-one conversation with the prospect. This is two-way communication. Now we are talking about a huge improvement in our results.

More examples.

* "Retired teachers only."

Teachers are great. They already know how to train people. And if they are retired, they have lots of time. Plus, maybe they'd like additional income beyond their pensions.

* "To people who hate their jobs."

This message will target those prospects who know they want something different in their lives. You can now offer them another option.

* "If your retirement pay is less than you'd like, read on."

Yes, almost every retiree would qualify, but only the people who want more retirement income will contact you. Again, this is more effective sorting, and you'll only attract interested prospects.

* "Professional trainers only."

You might get responses from corporate trainers, personal fitness trainers, or even sales trainers. You are targeting prospects that already have the most important skills for duplication: training skills.

* "Only three training positions remaining. Ready to train part-time for a new, better-paying career?"

This targets people stuck in a dead-end career. In addition, it offers them a chance to learn while they keep their present job. These prospects like the safety your offer provides.

#42. Sponsor a Fun Run.

Fun Runs are always looking for sponsors. Organizing events like these can be expensive. You can be a sponsor for a running event for as little as $50, and pay all the way up to $50,000 for a huge event.

Most of the time you will lose money, even if you only pay $50 for a small event. Few people will buy your product or join your business because they saw a logo on the back of a shirt or banner. Sure, the logo or banner looks good, but it won't be a good return on your investment.

Many of these running events raise money for a local cause or charity. So for them, any amount of sponsorship money is important, no matter how small.

Here's how you can help.

Most running events have packets for the runners, containing their T-shirts and a few miscellaneous items. What if you offered to put a flyer about your product in their packets? You could offer to give your profits to the charity they choose.

If they are looking to raise money, their cost is zero and there is no risk. You could even help them stuff the packets before the event.

Want to leverage this further?

What if you offered to give your profits to the cause or charity in exchange for a free booth at the event? That's another no-risk option for the charity. You could even advertise at your booth that you are helping raise money for the charitable cause. It is a win-win, and now the Fun Run organizers have a reason to promote your booth for you.

Let's take this another step further.

You could become a hero to the charity by finding more small business people like you, who would be willing to put their brochures and samples into the running event packets. Many small businesses wouldn't want to be a sponsor and buy an expensive booth. However, they would take this no-risk approach to finding new customers for their businesses.

#43. How to build a downline in a foreign market.

I was on an airplane with my longtime friend, Russ Noland. I asked him how he expanded his network into Germany. He said:

"I didn't know anyone in Germany, so I ran a local ad with the headline, 'Do you speak German?'

"Now I have a local lead with contacts in Germany."

Sometimes the solutions are simple.

How else could you find leads for foreign markets?

Let's say you live in Chicago and your company just opened into Japan. How are you going to build a downline in Japan when you don't have a single lead or contact in that country?

Here are some traditional ways that often fail:

1. Buy some names, addresses, phone numbers and email addresses of potential opportunity seekers and networkers in Japan. Contact them directly. And what happens?

Usually nothing. These cold leads don't know you, don't know about your opportunity, and they won't trust a cold-calling salesman from Chicago.

2. Buy an airline ticket to Japan. Get off the plane and aggressively stalk strangers and force them to listen to your sales pitch (in a foreign language). This doesn't work too well in Chicago where everyone speaks English, so it will certainly have its challenges in a foreign country.

So what can we do?

We need to find prospects who understand us and trust us. We need local prospects who have contacts in Japan. So where will we find these contacts? Try these two methods to start the creative thinking process.

1. Visit some of the local Japanese restaurants in Chicago. Buy a glass fish bowl and offer to place it near the cash register. Ask the manager if customers can place their business cards in the bowl to win a free lunch. Once a week, you can draw the winning business card. Now you have a great mailing list to announce your company's opening in Japan. Certainly some of these Japanese food enthusiasts will have contacts in Japan. Plus, it is a great way to get referrals.

2. Or from home, check the list of associations that cater to Japanese interests. Is there a small Japanese-language newspaper in the area? Would some of the martial arts clubs have contacts in Japan? Are there Facebook groups that cater to Japanese-American interests?

See the difference a little imagination can make?

The mailing list and airline methods cost money, lots of money. They also carry a high risk of failure.

The restaurant and association methods cost very little. And, you have a genuine chance of successfully finding good prospects and referrals for your business.

#44. Have your products delivered to your job.

If you order products from your network marketing company regularly, try this.

Always have your products delivered to your office, not to your home. When you open the box, you will be surrounded by curious co-workers. Expect to take some orders. Or at least expect to answer some questions.

If you wanted more interest, then order products twice a month. Start a little buzz or conversation at the office. Most co-workers are bored there anyway.

And if you have a catalog, make sure to leisurely page through your catalog looking for interesting things to order.

#45. Throw a promotion party!

If you have a local distributor group, here is a great way to bond, socialize, and motivate your group.

* If you've just qualified to be a platinum director, throw a platinum director party.

* If one of your distributors qualifies as a senior manager, throw a senior manager party.

* If one of your distributors qualifies as a diamond executive consultant, throw a diamond executive consultant party.

This is a great excuse to get your group together to bond, to give recognition, and to challenge the group to reach new positions in your business.

It is easier and more fun to get your distributors to a party than it is to get them to a meeting.

Then, tell your distributors to bring their friends to the party with them. Make it a big party with lots of "prospects" attending. They will want to know more about the promotion, the bonus check, the upcoming trips … and who knows? Maybe they will want to join your business just because they enjoyed hanging out with positive people who are more fun than their negative in-laws.

But, don't stop there …

Have more parties!

As the host or organizer, you will find it much easier to approach and visit with fellow partygoers.

What other types of parties can you promote? How about:

A class reunion party.

It doesn't have to be a five-year or ten-year reunion party. It could be a three-year reunion party. Or, you could just ask your classmates to come celebrate the seven-year anniversary of the big football game.

Don't limit your invitation to just your classmates. What about other classes? Or the teachers? Or the parents? Or the hot lunch staff?

You can find plenty of people to invite. And make sure that everyone fills in the guest book with their name, contact information, present occupation, etc. This will be helpful when you send a follow-up newsletter to the attendees.

A neighborhood party.

Organize a block party, a street cleanup party, or just a get-to-know-you party to meet the neighbors. It is inexpensive if you ask everyone to bring something to eat or drink.

At the very least, you will make some new friends in your neighborhood.

A party for your fellow employees.

These prospects have the same problems and dreams that you do. They work in the same environment. And it is easy to invite this group because you see them every day.

Don't limit your thinking to just your fellow employees. Consider that they will bring spouses or friends. Again, keep it simple. Keep the cost low. And get ready for the conversation that starts with:

"Oh, I hate my job. I am thinking of doing something different."

#46. How to get 300+ prospects willing to listen to you.

Warning: The following strategy will only work if you are a long-term player in network marketing.

Here is the strategy. Every day this year talk with one person. Simply say:

"I just realized a year of my life went right by me. Nothing changed. I am not going to waste another year of my life. What about you?"

Well, most people will let yet another year go by without any changes.

One year later, on the same day, go to that person and say this:

"Hey, remember last year when we said we weren't going to let another year of our life pass us by? Well, I got serious. I made some big changes. Glad I did. What about you?"

Now you have a prospect who just saw a year of his life wasted. This prospect is a bit more open-minded and wants to do something this year.

And you have 365 of these ready-to-go prospects to talk to.

All you have to do is keep a notebook of who you talked to and when. Then, one year from now you will have a great year with plenty of motivated prospects to talk to.

#47. The best people.

Who are the best potential prospects for your network marketing business? Which characteristics give some prospects the edge?

We, as network marketing professionals, should never prejudge an individual. We would check for their interest and desire first. However, we can grow faster if we can isolate success characteristics of the great leaders in network marketing. Let's do a little exercise that can help us isolate those characteristics.

Imagine the perfect network marketing leader. What would he or she be? An engineer? An accountant? A salesman? A business owner? How would you rank those professions? Which profession would be at the top of your list?

Now, let's look at the #1 duty of successful network marketing leaders: **Training.**

If we are to duplicate ourselves, we must become effective trainers. This is the key to building large and successful organizations. New prospects don't know the skills of our profession just because they completed an online application.

So, who are the greatest trainers?

Teachers!

Teachers practice their training skills all the time. They are patient, they know how to talk to people, they are willing to present information over and over again until their students "get it." They already have the skills to train new distributors to be successful when approaching and talking to prospects.

And what do new downline distributors want? A patient, skilled, empathetic trainer. Doesn't that describe a teacher?

Plus, teachers are notoriously underpaid! They can appreciate the opportunity of being fairly compensated for their skills. A network marketing opportunity can give them the cash flow needed to continue in their chosen profession, or to retire early.

Who are the best teachers? **Band teachers!**

If you've ever heard a grade-school or middle-school band, you know that band teachers have the ultimate patience. But wait!

Not only do band teachers have the patience and training skills, they also have great promotional skills. They raise money for band instruments, uniforms and trips. They have the sales ability of the greatest salesmen mixed with the training professionalism of the teacher. This is a perfect combination for the true network marketing leader.

If you jumped out of an airplane into a brand-new city, your first words might be,

"Take me to your band teachers!"

Now, what about salesmen? How do they rank?

What is the stereotype image of the average salesman? We often picture a hustler or peddler who pressures a customer into buying something he doesn't need. Then, the salesman quickly runs on to the next prospect while leaving his original customer orphaned forever. All that interests this salesman is how to make the next sale with someone new. Follow-up and service? Not in his vocabulary.

Does this sound like your network marketing leader profile?

This type of salesman has precisely the wrong skills needed to be an effective and successful network marketing leader! New distributors need follow-up, patience and training. They don't need an absentee leader.

When people ask you if you have to be a salesman to be a successful network marketing leader, you can answer,

"Only if you want to start with a handicap."

So, look for your potential leaders from individuals who have the patience to train their groups. Of course, there are good salesmen and bad salesmen, good teachers and bad teachers. Don't just look exclusively in certain professions, but look for the characteristics that make successful network marketing leaders.

51 Ways and Places
To Sponsor New Distributors

#48. The people you know.

Are relatives and friends hard to sponsor?

Relatives know us too well. They remember every mistake we made in the past and keep an organized diary of our mishaps. Relatives won't listen to us, they don't respect us, and they don't want to join our business.

Relatives are not good prospects.

Or, are they?

Do you realize that every network marketer in the world is somebody's relative? That's right! They must be a relative of someone. Now, they may not be your relative, but they are related to somebody.

The same holds true with friends. Everybody is somebody's friend. So friends make excellent network marketing distributors also.

Your distributor might say, "Relatives are no good. You can't sponsor relatives into network marketing."

But what is your distributor really saying?

"I can't sponsor my relatives. They hate me. They don't respect me. They want to see first if I am successful before they join. I haven't learned the skills to feel comfortable

139

presenting my program. I feel I must sell them something instead of letting them choose what is best for them. I am afraid of rejection. And, the entire gene pool that affects my relatives is, well ... defective."

Looks like your new distributor is refusing to take responsibility for his business. He is looking for people and things to blame for his failure. You can guarantee failure if the new distributor doesn't let anyone know about his business. You can't keep it top secret and expect your business to grow.

You can't blame your lack of success on relatives.

It doesn't matter who they are related to. What does matter is if the network business opportunity is something that can benefit others, not just you. Our only obligation is to let them know that the opportunity is available. They can refuse the opportunity, refuse to even listen to the presentation, or even refuse to know what the business opportunity is all about.

Again, our only obligation is to let people know that an opportunity exists. If they feel they have a need to check it out, that is great. Then they can decide if network marketing can help them achieve their dreams. They will make the decision based on what they want and need, not what we want or what some other relative wants. It is a personal decision.

So, don't worry if they are a relative or a friend. It is usually to our advantage. At least a relative or a friend is somebody we can talk to. They are a bit easier to contact than a total stranger. And usually, they will at least trust us enough to check out our business. That is all we ask.

So don't go around saying that you can't recruit relatives and friends. It is not your job to recruit them. Your duty is only to educate them if they request more information.

"But I don't want to talk to my friends and relatives until I am already successful."

On one of our annual MLM cruises, Orjan Saele of Norway shared this tip:

"Your warm market prospects are the most likely to join, so why call those least likely to join?"

This is a great statement to get your new distributors to contact their warm market first. Too often your new distributors want to run Internet ads, rent lists, and contact cold leads before they have the skills to present the opportunity properly.

Your new distributors have more rapport with their warm market. Their warm market will be more forgiving and most times will at least listen to what they have to offer. Cold prospects guard themselves from salespeople, and they don't want to spend time with beginners who haven't practiced their presentations yet.

#49. Make sure your business card "sells."

Most business cards end up in the nearest trash basket. They are boring. Do you really think your potential prospects have this sort of conversation at breakfast with their spouses?

Prospect: "I hope I get a business card today with a cute logo that I don't understand."

Spouse: "I hope I see a business card with a name of a company I really don't care about."

Prospect: "Well, if I am lucky today, I will get a business card with a name of a person I don't care about."

Spouse: "Gee, maybe I can get a business card that has a telephone number that I will never call."

Prospect: "Maybe I can collect a business card today with little tiny print I can't read."

Spouse: "Wouldn't it be wonderful if I could get a business card today with an email address that I can't figure out?"

Want more prospects to read and keep your business card or coupon?

Idea #1.

If you have a business card, and currently use a coupon to make a product or opportunity offer, try this. Make your coupon the entire back of your business card. People will keep your card because it is a coupon for a special offer or price discount.

Make a strong offer for your product or opportunity.

For example, your business card could say:

• $5 off SuperVitamins.

• First-time customers only.

• Free admission to business seminar.

• Present this ticket at the door.

• Free audio report.

• How to get an extra paycheck every week.

Business cards are cheap, cheaper than printing cheap-looking paper coupons. So when your next prospect asks you for a business card, give them your business card coupon with an offer they can't refuse.

Idea #2.

Print the back of your business card with your selling message ... backwards. Or print the entire text of the coupon backwards. Then instruct the prospect to hold your business card or coupon up to a mirror to read the offer.

This curiosity approach compels the prospect to read your message.

Idea #3.

Make the back of your business card a resource they want to keep. Of course many business cards have a calendar. That's boring. One salesman filled the back of his business card with telephone numbers of some very important people. He had the telephone numbers of the president, the Pope, the chief of police, the fire department, the local beautician, and of course his own telephone number too. Prospects kept his card as a conversation piece.

Idea #4.

Create a reason for the prospect to want to call you. How? By printing a great benefit on the back of your business card. For example:

* Free sample of the world's best-tasting healthy snack.

* Free list of the five best ways to fire your boss.

* Quick list of the best vacations for families.

* $50 cash back by using our service, plus save monthly too!

If you've already invested a fortune into business cards and don't want to buy more, then go to the local office supply store and get some inexpensive peel-and-stick labels for the back of your card.

Idea #5.

Our friend, Dayle, would always pass out his business cards each time he went to the grocery store. Even though he was a full-time networker and could go any time he pleased to the store, he always made it a point to go to the grocery store when it was the most crowded.

Then, he would always shop backwards. Usually the store flow starts the shoppers in the produce area, but he always started at the other end of the store and shopped the produce last. He found a way to "run into" more prospects.

While shopping he would lightly "run into" other grocery carts and say, "Whoops, looks like we got into an accident. If you see any damage, here is my card."

Most of the time he at least got a smile. He makes the world a better place and finds prospects too.

Don't keep your business cards for your grandchildren.

Your grandchildren want the money earned from passing out your business cards, not the business cards. So get your business cards out of the box and into the hands of prospects. Your cards work better when prospects actually have your cards.

#50. How to get more local prospects.

Years ago, I was sitting with Lisa Wilbur on the annual MLM cruise. She shared how she gets lots of local publicity, and brands her name into the minds of people.

Every election, she runs for state representative in her state of New Hampshire.

As the underdog, she gets plenty of local publicity, front page coverage, and she talks about her company (what she currently does for a living) in every interview. She has become quite the local celebrity and everyone knows about her company and her products.

Newspapers and radio stations love a good story. Underdogs with no campaign financing, trying to upset the political machines, make interesting stories.

She has lost the election five straight times.

Yes, she is a five-time loser, but she doesn't run for office to get a job. She runs for office to get the free publicity and branding. I think she secretly hopes she never comes close to winning as that would interfere with her lifestyle.

So how much did it cost Lisa to run for office?

At the time, only a $2 registration fee at the local town hall.

Lisa does many other amazing local prospecting and publicity campaigns, but running for office certainly caught my attention.

#51. Who sells to my prospects?

Here is another chance to think creatively.

First, mentally picture your ideal prospect. Where does your prospect go to work? What kinds of activities does your prospect enjoy? Where can you find places where groups of your prospects gather?

Second, ask yourself, "Who comes into contact with my prospect on a daily or regular basis?"

Once you complete these two steps, it is easy. Here are some examples of this exercise.

Finding thirsty prospects.

If you sell water filters, ask yourself the question: "Who sells to my potential water filter customers?" Then, start making your list of people who already have relationships with your potential customers.

You might befriend the bottled water truck driver as he makes deliveries.

Or, why not get to know the coffee salesman as he visits his office customers? If the office workers enjoy good coffee, they will want good-tasting water too.

What about the salesman who furnishes honor-system snacks to offices? How about the office supply salesman?

These are just a few good people who come in contact with our potential water filter prospects.

If we don't want to make personal sales calls, we can give these salesmen a brochure, coupon or a certificate that offers free filtered water at home for two weeks. This will pre-qualify and pre-sell our prospects.

A good headline for your brochure could be:

Filtered Water: Only 10 Cents A Gallon!
First 50 Gallons Free!

We have only looked at the business or office market so far. What about the residential market? Many people would want a water filter in their home.

But who are these hot, qualified residential prospects?

Hmm. If the homeowner purchases an air filtration system, wouldn't that homeowner want clean water also? Let's find the air filter dealer in our area.

If the homeowner takes vitamins, pure water would be a natural purchase. Now we are looking for the vitamin salesman.

What about the plumber? Or the handyman? They could easily make a recommendation for our water filter on one of their service calls.

It gets easier the longer we think from this perspective.

Let's take an extreme example
of a narrow product line.

A network marketing company invents an expensive oil additive that doubles the mileage on 1976 Volkswagens only. The motor vehicle record department won't give the network marketing distributor a mailing list of 1976 Volkswagen owners. What does the network marketing distributor do?

First, he contacts all the local repair garages. The distributor presents gift certificates that are good for one oil treatment on 1976 Volkswagens. Once the Volkswagen owner sees the mileage increase, reorders of the oil additive will be easy.

Second, the distributor gives certificates to local Volkswagen dealer service departments.

Third, every car insurance agency receives one free dinner at a local restaurant for every 1976 Volkswagen they insure. Their policy owner (the Volkswagen owner) gets a free dinner and a sales presentation for the oil additive.

Fourth, the local motor club salesman gets theater tickets for each membership sold to 1976 Volkswagen owners.

Fifth, the receptionist at the local bank that finances used cars receives flowers and movie tickets whenever she refers a customer who uses the special oil additive coupon.

Sixth, the local car wash crew gets a free pizza for every 1976 Volkswagen they spot if they get the owner's name and address.

Seventh, used car dealers and new car dealers (they take trade-ins) are contacted.

Hey, this is getting easier!

Even chubby people can't hide!

Charles and Kare Possick tell the story of finding qualified prospects for a weight-loss seminar. They had a client in the Los Angeles area who wanted to give lectures on how to lose weight.

They chose a direct mailing campaign as the most effective way to fill the lecture rooms for this project. When Charles and Kare tried to rent appropriate mailing lists, no one would share their prospecting lists. The national weight-loss companies would be in direct competition with these seminars, so everyone was reluctant to share or rent their lists.

The competition wouldn't budge. So, how did Charles and Kare find a suitable mailing list of prospects? They applied the marketing technique, "Who sells to my customers?"

Charles and Kare surmised that overweight women still bought pantyhose. And many of them purchased their pantyhose by mail. They contacted the list agent and were able to rent the names of all the women in the Los Angeles area that had purchased queen-sized pantyhose by mail.

Each of the 30,000 names on that list received an offer for a free ticket to the seminars, drawing 1,200 attendees.

Yes, a single mailing filled the seminar rooms. But more importantly, they filled the seminar rooms with highly-qualified, overweight prospects for their client's lectures. If you are going to speak to a room full of people, why not make sure they are eager and willing potential buyers of your products and services?

You don't have to harass dentists
to reach your prospects.

A network marketing company introduced a new dental product in Australia.

Who did the distributors contact? Every dentist in the country.

Unfortunately, there are not a lot of dentists in Australia. That meant that each dentist interrupted his day five or six times to answer the telephone to hear the same sales pitch from an eager distributor.

Soon the dentists were complaining to the trade organization. That's bad public relations for the network marketing industry.

So how did the smart distributors sell their new dental product?

They contacted school nurses.

School nurses were great contacts because they:

* See lots of teeth.

* Are trusted by parents to make recommendations.

* Have a steady stream of potential customers.

* Are underpaid and appreciate the opportunity to earn extra money.

"Who else comes into contact with my potential customers?"

* A specialty hair shampoo and conditioner network marketing distributor offers a discount coupon to give away with purse-size travel mirrors.

* The self-improvement network marketing distributor watches who checks out the positive mental attitude books at the local library and bookstores.

* The vitamin distributor makes friends with the exercise machine salesman, who sells to people concerned about their health.

One of my favorite campaigns.

While eating Mexican food with distributors from a workshop, I asked the lady across the table what she sold. She answered, "I sell diet products."

To continue the conversation, I asked, "So how is it going?"

She told me, "I am so tired. Every day I am delivering boxes and boxes of my diet products to customers all over the city. This is exhausting."

Now, I am thinking, "That is pretty incredible. She must have a secret. Maybe the diet products are a bargain or something."

So I asked her, "Well, how much do these diet products cost?"

She said, "Well, the cheapest package is $350 for a month's supply, but I normally sell the $600 packs."

I now think, "$600 a pack? I could buy 300 baskets of these tortilla chips for that. That is expensive for a month of diet products. How could she sell that many packs so easily?" But, I kept my composure and posture.

I then asked, "So tell me. Where do you find these prospects for those expensive $600 diet packs? Let me know and maybe I could give you some advice or a tip or two."

Her reply sums up why it is important to know, "Who sells to my prospects?"

She said:

"I go to bridal shows and talk to the brides-to-be. When I ask them if they want to lose a little weight before the wedding, they instantly say 'Yes.' This is their big day. No matter how anorexic-looking the bride-to-be appears, every bride wants to lose just a little more weight before their special day.

"The average wedding costs between $20,000 and $50,000 here. The $600 diet pack isn't even a thought, it is barely a tip. So the bride-to-be orders immediately, no questions asked.

"But then the bride's mother decides that she wants to lose weight too. She doesn't want to look fat in those wedding pictures for the rest of eternity. She orders her pack.

"And so does the future mother-in-law. She doesn't want to be the fat one in the picture.

"And then, the bridesmaids. They are already going to look awful in those off-color dresses they have to wear to make the bride look pretty. They don't want to look awful and fat. They order too.

"So I load up my car with as many packs as I can, and I spend the entire day delivering and talking to my new, enthusiastic customers."

Needless to say, I didn't give her any advice or tips.

#52. Bonus! Just meet new people!

Not enough good quality prospects = **Stress!**

Scenario #1: When we only have a few prospects, we press, we push, we strain to make them join our opportunity. Prospects feel this pressure and instinctively back away from us. This leads to fewer prospects and the vicious cycle just gets worse.

Scenario #2: When we have an abundance of prospects, we are happy. We are not desperately waiting for a single decision from a single prospect.

We aren't married to the outcome of a single presentation. Instead, we relax and feel more confident, because we have many more prospects waiting for us.

We simply share our opportunity and take the first prospects who step forward. Now we are working with volunteers and we feel that we have more great prospects waiting in line.

Which scenario describes your career?

Are you pressing and struggling from too few prospects? Or, are you accepting applications from the best volunteers from your large pool of quality prospects?

The solution is simple.

Increase your marketing so that you have an abundance of prospects.

Why not increase your personal contacts now?

Here are some more quick ideas.

1. Offer to be a guest on a local radio talk show. (And yes, you can be an Internet radio talk show host too.) Or, just create an audio of great information that people want, and make it available as a podcast.

2. Loan out ten physical audios, videos or books about your business opportunity. Even if you are not very good yet at follow-up, the exposure may reach someone who is ready right now.

3. Pass out 10 product audios, videos or books, explaining the benefits of your product. If you excite a new customer, your new customer might know others who feel the same way.

4. Join a Meetup group in your area. Be creative in your choices. For instance, if you wanted to reach people near retirement age, who might want to supplement their pensions or retirement income, you might join a Meetup social group that owns RVs and travel trailers. Most cities have many different groups that meet monthly with a variety of interests.

5. Go to free seminars that talk about investing or careers. The people you meet at these seminars all want more in their lives. At the very least, you will make new friends with a common interest.

6. Take a class about something you are passionate about. It could be a writing class, a skydiving class, or a foreign language class. You will meet other people with similar interests, and who knows? Maybe they want more time to pursue their passions also.

7. Volunteer. Charity work is good. It makes the world a better place. Don't just join to search for prospects. Join to help. You naturally meet new people, and your personal network of friends will expand.

So when should you prospect for new distributors?

Prospecting is like going on a diet.

When would it be a good time to diet?

One day a year?

No, that would not be too successful. We may lose weight on the one day that we diet, but the other 364 days would cancel our one day of progress.

One day a month?

Again, our dieting is not consistent enough to be successful.

One day a week?

Better. But do you think you can lose weight by dieting only one day of the week?

Daily?

That is the key to success in dieting. Just a small effort on a daily basis will create the results we want.

And that is how leaders prospect.

They do a little bit each day. Distributors think leaders have some sort of secret trick that they perform to become successful. The truth is, leaders tend to be more consistent in their sponsoring efforts.

How can we teach our new distributors to have consistent results also?

How about asking them to choose one of the 50+ solutions in this book?

By actively expanding their network, soon they will have all the prospects they need for a successful network marketing business. No longer will they suffer from the stress of where to find the next good prospect. With plenty of prospects, their entire "positioning" changes from desperation to confidence.

A Zen saying, but it's not true!

"Sitting quietly, doing nothing, spring comes, and the grass grows by itself."

Maybe this works for the weather, but not for network marketing. I think the Zen philosophy is practiced by many network marketers. They get excited at the meeting, then go home and keep the opportunity "top secret" from their friends and family.

Use these 50+ prospecting ways to expand your business now.

FREE!

Get seven mini-reports of amazing, easy sentences that create new, hot prospects.

Discover how just a few correct words can change your network marketing results forever.

Get all seven free Big Al mini-reports, and the free weekly Big Al Report with more recruiting and prospecting tips.

Sign up today at:

http://www.BigAlReport.com

MORE BIG AL RESOURCES

Want Big Al to speak in your area?

Request a Big Al training event:

http://www.BigAlSeminars.com

See a full line of Big Al products at:

http://www.FortuneNow.com

MORE BIG AL BOOKS

The Four Color Personalities for MLM
The Secret Language for Network Marketers

Ice Breakers!
How To Get Any Prospect To Beg You For A Presentation

How To Get Instant Trust, Belief, Influence and Rapport!
13 Ways To Create Open Minds By Talking To The
Subconscious Mind

First Sentences for Network Marketing
How To Quickly Get Prospects On Your Side

Big Al's MLM Sponsoring Magic
How to Build a Network Marketing Team Quickly

How To Prospect, Sell And Build Your Network
Marketing Business With Stories

26 Instant Marketing Ideas To Build Your Network
Marketing Business

How To Build Network Marketing Leaders Volume One:
Step-By-Step Creation Of MLM Professionals

How To Build Network Marketing Leaders Volume Two:
Activities And Lessons For MLM Leaders

Start SuperNetworking! 5 Simple Steps To Creating Your
Own Personal Networking Group

How to Follow Up With Your Network Marketing
Prospects: Turn Not Now Into Right Now!

http://www.BigAlBooks.com

ABOUT THE AUTHORS

Keith Schreiter has 20+ years of experience in network marketing and MLM. As the co-author of *How to Follow Up With Your Network Marketing Prospects: Turn Not Now Into Right Now* and *Start SuperNetworking! 5 Simple Steps to Creating Your Own Personal Networking Group*, Keith shows network marketers how to use simple systems to build a stable and growing business.

So, do you need more prospects? Do you need your prospects to commit instead of stalling? Want to know how to engage and keep your group active? If these are the types of skills you would like to master, you will enjoy his "how-to" style.

Keith speaks and trains in the U.S., Canada, and Europe.

Tom "Big Al" Schreiter has 40+ years of experience in network marketing and MLM. As the author of the original "Big Al" training books in the late '70s, he has continued to speak in over 80 countries on using the exact words and phrases to get prospects to open up their minds and say "YES."

His passion is marketing ideas, marketing campaigns, and how to speak to the subconscious mind in simplified, practical ways. He is always looking for case studies of incredible marketing campaigns that give usable lessons.

As the author of numerous audio trainings, Tom is a favorite speaker at company conventions and regional events.

14562885R00092

Printed in Great Britain
by Amazon.co.uk, Ltd.,
Marston Gate.